Section 1983 Litigation

Karen M. Blum
Suffolk University Law School

Kathryn R. Urbonya
The College of William & Mary School of Law

Federal Judicial Center 1998

This Federal Judicial Center publication was undertaken in furtherance of the Center's statutory mission to conduct and stimulate research and development for the improvement of judicial administration. The views expressed are those of the authors and not necessarily those of the Federal Judicial Center.

Contents

Preface

This monograph analyzes the fundamental issues that arise in litigation under 42 U.S.C. § 1983, the statute for redressing constitutional and federal statutory violations, and the case law interpreting those issues. Research for this first edition concluded with the 1997–1998 Supreme Court term.

For a more in-depth treatment of § 1983 lawsuits, one should consult two leading treatises: *Section 1983 Litigation* (3d ed. 1997), by Martin A. Schwartz and John E. Kirklin, and *Civil Rights and Civil Liberties Litigation* (4th ed. 1998), by Sheldon H. Nahmod.

We would like to thank Judge Rya W. Zobel, director of the Federal Judicial Center, Judge Thomas F. Hogan (District of the District of Columbia), Judge Virginia M. Morgan (Eastern District of Michigan), and Magistrate Judge Jacob Hagopian (District of Rhode Island) for reviewing drafts of this manuscript. We also deeply appreciate the excellent editorial support from Kris Markarian of the FJC.

Chapter 1

Introduction to Constitutional Torts Litigation

Title 42, § 1983 of the U.S. Code provides a mechanism for seeking redress for an alleged deprivation of a litigant's federal constitutional and federal statutory rights by persons acting under color of state law. Section 1983 reads as follows:

> Every person who, under color of any statute, ordinance, regulation, custom, or usage, of any state or territory, subjects, or causes to be subjected, any citizen of the United States or other person within the jurisdiction thereof to the deprivation of any rights, privileges, or immunities secured by the Constitution and laws, shall be liable to the party injured in an action at law, suit in equity, or other proper proceeding for redress, except that in any action brought against a judicial officer for an act or omission taken in such officer's judicial capacity, injunctive relief shall not be granted unless a declaratory decree was violated or declaratory relief was unavailable. For the purposes of this section, any Act of Congress applicable exclusively to the District of Columbia shall be considered to be a statute of the District of Columbia. [1]

Litigating under this statute is complex. Through the years, the Supreme Court has been able to interpret the terms "person," "under color of law," "subjects, or causes to be subjected," and "and laws." However, the statute "provides little or no guidance regarding important subjects such as the measure of damages, availability of punitive damages, requirements for equitable relief, statute of limitations, survival of claims,

---

1. 42 U.S.C. § 1983 (1996).

1

proper parties, and immunities from suit."[2] In an attempt to resolve these issues, the Court has taken steps to examine congressional intent, common-law practices, policy concerns, federalism issues, and comity problems.

History

Congress passed 42 U.S.C. § 1983 in 1871 as section 1 of the "Ku Klux Klan Act." The statute did not emerge as a tool for checking the abuse by state officials, however, until 1961, when the Supreme Court decided *Monroe v. Pape*.[3] In *Monroe*, the Court articulated three purposes for passage of the statute: (1) "to override certain kinds of state laws"; (2) to provide "a remedy where state law was inadequate"; and (3) to provide "a federal remedy where the state remedy, though adequate in theory, was not available in practice."[4]

The *Monroe* Court resolved two important issues that allowed 42 U.S.C. § 1983 to become a powerful statute for enforcing rights secured by the Fourteenth Amendment. First, it held that actions taken by state governmental officials, even if contrary to state law, were nevertheless actions taken "under color of law." Second, the Court held that injured individuals have a federal remedy under 42 U.S.C. § 1983 even if the officials' actions also violated state law. In short, the statute was intended to provide a supplemental remedy. The federal forum was necessary to vindicate federal rights because, according to Congress in 1871, state courts could not protect Fourteenth Amendment rights because of their "prejudice, passion, neglect, [and] intolerance."[5]

With *Monroe* opening the door to the federal courthouse, constitutional litigation against state officials developed. Later, plaintiffs seeking monetary damages sued not only state officials but began to sue cities and counties as well. They also sought prospective injunctive relief against state officials. Ultimately, the federal court became the place to reform state governmental practices.

---

2. Jack M. Beerman, *A Critical Approach to Section 1983 with Special Attention to Sources of Law*, 42 Stan. L. Rev. 51 (1989).

3. 365 U.S. 167 (1961).

4. *Id.* at 173–75.

5. *Id.* at 180.

Jurisdiction

Two jurisdictional statutes apply to 42 U.S.C. § 1983 litigation in federal court: 28 U.S.C. § 1343(a)(3),[6] the jurisdictional counterpart of 42 U.S.C. § 1983; and 28 U.S.C. § 1331,[7] the general federal question statute. Of the two statutes, § 1331 provides for more expansive jurisdiction because it affords jurisdiction in cases raising a federal question. In contrast, § 1343(a)(3) limits federal jurisdiction to suits involving "equal rights." Neither statute sets an amount that must be in controversy for jurisdiction to attach.

With jurisdiction over federal claims, many federal courts in 42 U.S.C. § 1983 suits also have jurisdiction to adjudicate state law claims that arise out of "a common nucleus of operative fact."[8] Formerly known as ancillary and pendent jurisdiction, supplemental jurisdiction under 28 U.S.C. § 1367 permits both pendent claim and pendent party jurisdiction.[9] 28 U.S.C. § 1367 changed "the preexisting law in that it makes supplemental jurisdiction mandatory, not discretionary."[10]

---

6. 28 U.S.C. § 1343(a)(3) (1993) provides as follows:

> (a) The district courts shall have original jurisdiction of any civil action authorized by law to be commenced by any person: . . . (3) To redress the deprivation, under color of any State law, statute, ordinance, regulation, custom or usage, of any right, privilege or immunity secured by the Constitution of the United States or by any Act of Congress providing for equal rights of citizens or of all persons within the jurisdiction of the United States.

7. 28 U.S.C. § 1331 (1993) provides that "district courts shall have original jurisdiction of all civil actions arising under the Constitution, laws or treaties of the United States."

8. United Mine Workers v. Gibbs, 383 U.S. 715, 725 (1966).

9. 28 U.S.C. § 1367(a) (1993) provides as follows:

> [I]n any civil action of which the district courts have original jurisdiction, the district courts shall have supplemental jurisdiction over all other claims that are so related to claims in the action within such original jurisdiction that they form part of the same case or controversy under Article III of the United States Constitution. Such supplemental jurisdiction shall include claims that involve the joinder or intervention of additional parties.

10. Erwin Chemerinsky, Federal Jurisdiction, § 5.4, at 317 (2d ed. 1994). The district court *may decline* to exercise supplemental jurisdiction in the following circumstances:

> (1) the claim raises a novel or complex issue of state law;
> (2) the claim substantially predominates over the claim or claims over which the district court has original jurisdiction;
> (3) the district court has dismissed all claims over which it has original jurisdiction;
> (4) in exceptional circumstances, where there are other compelling reasons for declining jurisdiction.

28 U.S.C. § 1367(b) (1993).

Prima Facie Case

To establish a prima facie case under 42 U.S.C. § 1983, plaintiffs must allege two elements: (1) the action occurred "under color of law" and (2) the action is a deprivation of a constitutional right or a federal statutory right.[11] The first element, discussed in Chapter 2, *infra*, involves a fact-specific inquiry wherein the court must examine the relationship between the challenged action and the government. The second element is explained in Chapters 3, 4, and 5, which deal with the First, Fourth, Eighth, and Fourteenth Amendments.

---

11. Parratt v. Taylor, 451 U.S. 527, 535 (1981).

Chapter 2

Action "Under Color of Law"

Title 42, § 1983 of the U.S. Code imposes liability only upon those individuals and entities that act "under color of law." In the typical § 1983 case, the under-color-of-law inquiry is not difficult because plaintiffs sue governmental employees and entities for conduct pursuant to their governmental duties and powers.[12] However, when plaintiffs sue private actors who are "linked" to state officials in different ways, many courts[13] and scholars[14] have struggled to distinguish between private action and action under color of law. In response, the Supreme Court has articulated two guideposts. First, any state action under the Fourteenth Amendment is action under color of law.[15] Second, when the defendant is not a government employee, but is somehow linked to the government, courts

---

12. Tennessee v. Garner, 471 U.S. 1, 5–7 (1985) (police officer and city were sued for use of deadly force) (discussed *infra* text accompanying notes 135–38).

13. *See, e.g.,* Lebron v. National R.R. Passenger Corp., 115 S. Ct. 961, 964 (1995) (stating that "[i]t is fair to say that 'our cases deciding when private action might be deemed that of the state have not been a model of consistency'") (quoting Edmonson v. Leesville Concrete Co., 500 U.S. 614, 632 (1991) (O'Connor, J., dissenting)).

14. Laurence H. Tribe, American Constitutional Law, § 81-1, at 1609 (2d ed. 1988) ("the Supreme Court has not succeeded in developing a body of state action 'doctrine,' a set of rules for determining whether governmental or private actors are to be deemed responsible for an asserted constitutional violation").

15. West v. Atkins, 487 U.S. 42, 49–50 (1988); Lugar v. Edmondson Oil Co., 457 U.S. 922, 935 (1982). Action "under color of law," however, would not constitute state action if a court were to interpret the "under color of law" element to mean that the person merely acted "'with the knowledge of and pursuant to [a] statute.'" *Id.* at 935 n.18 (quoting Adickes v. Kress & Co., 398 U.S. 144, 162 n.23 (1970)).

must question whether there was joint action, an intertwined relationship, state encouragement, or a public function performed.[16]

When a plaintiff sues a governmental entity, such as a city or county, for a constitutional violation arising from its policy or custom, action under color of law is present because the entity was created by state law.[17] A corporation can be a governmental entity if the government created it to further its objectives and retains permanent control over it.[18] Because a governmental entity acts only through its agents or employees, under most circumstances, its employees also act under color of law.

Government employees act under color of law when performing their duties, whether they act in compliance with state law, contrary to it,[19] or exercise professional discretion.[20] Actions pursuant to state law easily reveal the link between the employee and the state. Actions contrary to state law are also actions under color of law because employees are given the power to act on behalf of the government.[21] Similarly, state employees or contractors who exercise professional judgment during the course of their employment act under color of law. Although the assertion of independent judgment may appear to suggest autonomy, professionals, such as prison physicians, exercise this judgment on behalf of the state,[22] in furtherance of the goals of the state.

In some circumstances, governmental employees do not act under color of law.[23] Public defenders, for example, although paid by the state to defend a criminal suspect,[24] act as an adversary to the state. The only link between the public defenders and the state is money. Joint action can exist, however, if public defenders conspire with other state officials

---

16. Martin A. Schwartz & John E. Kirklin, 1A Section 1983 Litigation: Claims & Defenses, § 5.10, at 520 (3d ed. 1997).

17. *See, e.g.,* Monell v. Department of Soc. Servs., 436 U.S. 658, 690–91 (1978).

18. *See Lebron,* 115 S. Ct. at 974 (holding that the National Passenger Corporation, known as "Amtrak," is a governmental entity created by Congress).

19. *See* Monroe v. Pape, 365 U.S. 167 (1961), *rev'd on other grounds,* Monell v. Department of Soc. Servs., 436 U.S. 658 (1978).

20. *West,* 487 U.S. at 49–50.

21. *Monroe,* 365 U.S. at 176, *rev'd on other grounds,* Monell v. Department of Soc. Servs., 436 U.S. 658 (1978).

22. *West,* 487 U.S. at 49–50.

23. Polk County v. Dodson, 451 U.S. 312, 325 (1981).

24. *Id.*

during the course of a criminal prosecution.[25] In this situation, there is a link between the "private" public defender and other state officials. Public defenders may also act under color of law when they perform administrative functions, such as hiring or firing employees, because such actions would be taken on behalf of the state, not in opposition to it.[26]

A more difficult under-color-of-law question arises when police officers, who act under color of law while on duty, are technically "off-duty." The key issues focus on the assertion of power and the actual power given them under state law. In determining whether the actions were under color of law, courts have considered the following ties to the state: whether the officers used the guns given to them by the state; whether the officers asserted authority given to them by their office; or whether their actions were ones that typically fall within the duties of police officers.[27] The more the facts link the actions of the officers with the power given to them by the state, the more likely that courts will find that they acted under color of law.

Governmental officials generally act under color of law because the state has given them the power to act; the link to the state is obvious. When individuals do not work for the government, the under-color-of-law inquiry still focuses on the connection between the challenged action and the government. The question becomes whether there is a sufficient link between the private individual and the state. The Supreme Court has articulated four related standards to determine whether there is a sufficient connection between the individual and the government such that the action by the individual nevertheless constitutes action by the government: joint actions, intertwined relationships, state encouragement, and public function.

Joint Actions

When the challenged action is committed by a person who does not work for the government, the under-color-of-law inquiry focuses on the nature of the connections between the private person and the state. Two common situations easily suggest actions under color of law. First, a private

---

25. Tower v. Glover, 467 U.S. 914, 919–20 (1984).

26. *Polk County*, 451 U.S. at 325.

27. Martin A. Schwartz & John E. Kirklin, 1A Section 1983 Litigation: Claims & Defenses, § 5.14, at 538–43 (3d ed. 1997) (collecting cases).

person who conspires with a state actor is a state actor for the purpose of the alleged conspiracy.[28] Second, a private person who acts as an agent of the state acts under color of law.[29] In the latter situation, action under color of law is present, even though the person is not a full-time employee of the state, because for purposes of the challenged action the person functions as if he or she were a full-time employee.

Intertwined Relationships

The Supreme Court has decided many cases involving the issue of when a private person is sufficiently intertwined with the state to have acted under color of law. Most of these cases require close scrutiny of the facts; under-color-of-law analysis is difficult to categorize because the Supreme Court has articulated the following "standard": "Only by sifting the facts and weighing the circumstances can the non-obvious involvement of the State in private conduct be attributed its true significance."[30] In each case, the Court's holding is necessarily limited because the under-color-of-law issue is a fact-specific inquiry. These decisions reveal the Court's movement toward limiting the circumstances under which a private person has become a state actor.

When evaluating the nexus between the private person and the state, the Court found the threshold for state action present when there was a symbiotic relationship. In *Burton v. Wilmington Parking Authority*,[31] the Supreme Court held that a private restaurant in a public building was a state actor when it refused to allow service to African-Americans. The Court detailed the symbiotic relationship between the restaurant and the state parking garage. The private restaurant was an integral part of the public building, not only in serving the public, but also in financing the public parking.

Since *Burton*, the Court has found numerous relationships to be insufficient to establish governmental action: these cases suggest that the link between the private person and the government must be obvious. The National Collegiate Athletic Association was not a state actor when it

---

28. Dennis v. Sparks, 449 U.S. 24, 28 (1980) (holding that private parties who corruptly conspired with a state judge acted "under color of law").

29. Adickes v. Kress & Co., 398 U.S. 144, 152 (1970) (stating that action is "under color" if person is a "wilful participant in joint activity with the State or its agents").

30. Burton v. Wilmington Parking Auth., 365 U.S. 715, 722 (1961).

31. 365 U.S. 715, 724 (1961).

persuaded the University of Nevada at Las Vegas to suspend its basketball coach;[32] the United States Olympic Committee was not a governmental actor when it refused to allow a nonprofit organization to use the word "olympic";[33] a private school for troubled students that received more than 90% of its funds from the government was not a governmental actor;[34] a private hospital that discharged patients early, according to its interpretation of Medicaid regulations, was not a governmental actor;[35] a utility that had a monopoly on electrical services was not a state entity;[36] and a private, racially discriminatory club that received a state liquor license was not a state actor.[37]

In the commercial litigation context, however, the Supreme Court has required fewer ties to the state when determining whether a private person acted under color of law. Although mere use of a state statute, alone, does not make the user a state actor,[38] when combined with the presence of state officials, it can signify state action.[39] In *Lugar v. Edmondson Oil Co.,*[40] the Supreme Court held that a creditor who used a state prejudgment statute had acted under color of law because, in attaching the debtor's property, with help from the court clerk and sheriff, the creditor had further used state power. The assistance from state officials made the creditor a joint participant in state action.[41]

Determining whether a private person acted jointly or was intertwined with a state actor thus requires analysis of all the links between the private person and the state. Except for the prejudgment attachment process, the Court has required obvious ties to the state. These ties must in

32. NCAA v. Tarkanian, 488 U.S. 179, 199 (1988) (the NCAA and the UNLV functioned more as adversaries rather than joint participants).

33. San Francisco Arts & Athletics v. United States Olympic Comm., 483 U.S. 522, 547 (1987).

34. Rendell-Baker v. Kohn, 457 U.S. 830, 841 (1982).

35. Blum v. Yaretsky, 457 U.S. 991, 1005 (1982).

36. Jackson v. Metropolitan Edison Co., 419 U.S. 345, 351 (1974).

37. Moose Lodge v. Irvis, 407 U.S. 163, 177–79 (1972).

38. Flagg Bros. v. Brooks, 436 U.S. 149, 164–66 (1978).

39. Lugar v. Edmondson Oil Co., 457 U.S. 922, 939–42 (1982).

40. 457 U.S. 922 (1982).

41. *Id.* at 937. The Court explained that in this context the alleged "deprivation must be caused by the exercise of some right or privilege created by the State or by a rule of conduct imposed by the state or by a person for whom the state is responsible." *Id.* In a footnote, the Supreme Court stated that its analysis was limited to prejudgment seizures of property. *Id.* at 939 n.21.

some way indicate that the state has done more than fund the private person's activities; they must suggest that the state has a significant measure of control over the private person's conduct.

State Encouragement

The Supreme Court has determined that state action is present when judges are asked to enforce or authorize a discriminatory practice.[42] Although application of the state encouragement doctrine does not generally arise in § 1983 lawsuits, the doctrine follows the contours of its state-action inquiry. This doctrine has been used, for example, to bar a court from enforcing a racially restrictive covenant[43] and allowing peremptory challenges to be used in a discriminatory manner.[44] In both these areas, the Court recognized that private discrimination would not be possible without judicial power. Because the use of judicial power in these contexts would sanction private discrimination, the Fourteenth Amendment prohibits judges from using their power in this manner.

Public Function

State action may be present if the private person is performing a function that is "the exclusive prerogative of the State."[45] In the landmark case, *Marsh v. Alabama*,[46] the Supreme Court held that a company that owned a town was a state actor when it barred the distribution of religious literature.[47] In later cases, however, the Supreme Court significantly narrowed *Marsh*, holding that the following activities are not public functions: operating a shopping mall,[48] providing utility services,[49] educating

---

42. *See, e.g.,* Edmonson v. Leesville Concrete Co., 500 U.S. 614, 627–28 (1991); Shelley v. Kraemer, 334 U.S. 1, 22–23 (1948).

43. *Shelley*, 334 U.S. at 22–23.

44. *Edmonson*, 500 U.S. at 627–28.

45. Jackson v. Metropolitan Edison Co., 419 U.S. 345, 353 (1974).

46. 326 U.S. 501, 508–09 (1946).

47. *Id.* at 508–09.

48. Hudgens v. NLRB, 424 U.S. 507, 520–21 (1976).

49. *Jackson*, 419 U.S. at 358–59.

troubled children,[50] and supporting nursing-home care.[51] Most federal courts have narrowly interpreted the public function standard.[52]

Thus, the question whether state action is present requires detailed analysis of the facts of each case. The state-action inquiry not only explores the links between the private person and the state, but also assesses the significance of each tie and the cumulative effect of the ties. This inquiry is not easily answered by studying Supreme Court decisions, and it ultimately invites judges to determine "where the governmental sphere ends and the private sphere begins."[53]

50. Rendell-Baker v. Kohn, 457 U.S. 830, 840–43 (1982).

51. Blum v. Yaretsky, 457 U.S. 991 (1982).

52. Martin A. Schwartz & John E. Kirklin, 1A Section 1983 Litigation: Claims & Defenses, § 5.14, at 538–43 (3d ed. 1997) (courts have held that the following are not public functions: providing health care, housing, legal services, and mass transportation).

53. *Edmonson*, 500 U.S. at 620.

Chapter 3

Deprivation of Selected Constitutional Rights

The due process clause of the Fourteenth Amendment encompasses three kinds of federal claims enforceable through 42 U.S.C. § 1983: (1) claims for the deprivation of certain specific rights denoted in the Bill of Rights and made applicable to the states through incorporation; (2) claims under the substantive component of the due process clause "that bars certain arbitrary, wrongful government actions, 'regardless of the fairness of the procedures used to implement them'"; and (3) claims under the procedural component of the due process clause that prohibits the deprivation of life, liberty, or property without fair procedure.[54]

When a plaintiff asserts the violation of a right specifically identified in the Bill of Rights or protected under the substantive component of the due process clause, the violation is complete at the time of the challenged conduct and the § 1983 remedy is available regardless of remedies provided under state law.[55] In addition to these Fourteenth Amendment rights, a violation of the dormant commerce clause is actionable under § 1983.[56] The following sections discuss some of the constitutional claims frequently litigated under § 1983.

Procedural Due Process Claims

A claim based on a denial of procedural due process challenges the constitutional adequacy of state law procedural protections accompanying

---

54. Zinermon v. Burch, 494 U.S. 113, 124 (1990) (quoting Daniels v. Williams, 474 U.S. 327, 331 (1986)).

55. *Id.* at 125.

56. Dennis v. Higgins, 498 U.S. 439, 450–51 (1991).

an alleged deprivation of a constitutionally protected interest in life, liberty, or property. It is not the deprivation itself that is actionable, but only the deprivation without the requisite process.

A court encountering a procedural due process claim must first determine whether the plaintiff has been deprived of a life, liberty, or property interest that is constitutionally protected as a matter of substantive law.[57] While liberty interests may be derived directly from the due process clause of the Constitution[58] or be created by state law,[59] property interests "are created from an independent source such as state law. . . ."[60]

In *Sandin v. Conner*,[61] the Supreme Court held, in the context of a procedural due process claim raised by an inmate placed in disciplinary segregation for thirty days, that, despite the mandatory language of the applicable prison regulation, a constitutionally protected liberty interest will generally be "limited to freedom from restraint which . . . imposes atypical and significant hardships on the inmate in relation to the ordinary incidents of prison life."[62] Under *Sandin*, mandatory language of a state prison regulation is still a necessary, but no longer a sufficient, prerequisite for finding a liberty interest. Courts must look to the substance of the deprivation and assess the hardship imposed on the inmate relative to the ordinary incidents of prison life.[63]

---

57. Cleveland Bd. of Educ. v. Loudermill, 470 U.S. 532, 541 (1985). *See, e.g.,* Paul v. Davis, 424 U.S. 693, 712 (1976) (holding that "the interest in reputation asserted in this case is neither 'liberty' nor 'property' guaranteed against state deprivation without due process of law").

58. *See, e.g.,* Washington v. Harper, 494 U.S. 210, 221–22 (1990) (due process clause confers on prisoners a liberty interest in being free from involuntary administration of psychotropic drugs); Vitek v. Jones, 445 U.S. 480, 493–94 (1980) (due process clause confers on prisoners a liberty interest in not being involuntarily committed to a state mental hospital).

59. Wolff v. McDonnell, 418 U.S. 539, 557 (1974) (state law created a liberty interest in a "shortened prison sentence" that resulted from good time credits).

60. *Cleveland Bd. of Educ.,* 470 U.S. at 538 (citing Board of Regents v. Roth, 408 U.S. 564, 577 (1972)).

61. 115 S. Ct. 2293 (1995).

62. *Id.* at 2300.

63. *See, e.g.,* Griffin v. Vaughn, 112 F.3d 703, 707 (3d Cir. 1997) (finding "exposure to the conditions of administrative custody for periods as long as 15 months 'falls within the expected parameters of the sentence imposed [on him] by a court of law'"); Brooks v. DiFasi, 112 F.3d 46, 49 (2d Cir. 1997) ("After *Sandin*, in order to determine whether a prisoner has a liberty interest in avoiding disciplinary confinement, a court must examine

Sandin did not disturb *Wolff v. McDonnell*,[64] which held that a state may create a liberty interest on the part of inmates in the accumulation of good conduct time credits.[65] Thus, if disciplinary action would inevitably affect the duration of the inmate's confinement, a liberty interest would still be recognized under *Wolff*.[66] Likewise, claims having their source in other than procedural due process, such as First Amendment retaliatory transfer or retaliatory discipline cases, are not affected by *Sandin*.[67]

Once a protected interest has been identified, a court must examine the process that accompanies the deprivation of that protected interest and decide whether the procedural safeguards built into the process are

the specific circumstances of the punishment."); Miller v. Selsky, 111 F.3d 7, 9 (2d Cir. 1997) ("*Sandin* did not create a per se blanket rule that disciplinary confinement may never implicate a liberty interest. Courts of appeals in other circuits have apparently come to the same conclusion, recognizing that district courts must examine the circumstances of a confinement to determine whether that confinement affected a liberty interest." (citing cases)); Dominique v. Weld, 73 F.3d 1156, 1159 (1st Cir. 1996) (finding no liberty interest in work release status); Bulger v. United States Bureau of Prisons, 65 F.3d 48, 50 (5th Cir. 1995) (holding no liberty interest in job assignment); Orellana v. Kyle, 65 F.3d 29, 31–32 (5th Cir. 1995) (suggesting that only deprivations "that clearly impinge on the duration of confinement, will henceforth qualify for constitutional liberty status"), *cert. denied*, 116 S. Ct. 736 (1996); Whitford v. Boglino, 63 F.3d 527, 533 (7th Cir. 1995) (observing that "[t]he holding in *Sandin* implies that states may grant prisoners liberty interests in being in the general population only if the conditions of confinement in segregation are significantly more restrictive than those in the general population").

64. 418 U.S. 539 (1974).

65. *Id.* Before being deprived of good-time credits an inmate must be afforded: (1) 24-hour advance written notice of the alleged violations; (2) the opportunity to be heard before an impartial decision maker; (3) the opportunity to call witnesses and present documentary evidence (when such presentation is consistent with institutional safety); and (4) a written decision by the fact-finder stating the evidence relied upon and the reasons for the disciplinary action. *Id.* at 563–71.

66. *See, e.g.,* Whitford v. Boglino, 63 F.3d 527, 532 (7th Cir. 1995). Note, however, that "the mere opportunity to earn good-time credits" has been held not to "constitute a constitutionally cognizable liberty interest sufficient to trigger the protection of the Due Process Clause." Luken v. Scott, 71 F.3d 192, 193–94 (5th Cir. 1995) (per curiam).

67. *See, e.g.,* Hines v. Gomez, 108 F.3d 265, 269 (9th Cir. 1997); Cornell v. Woods, 69 F.3d 1383, 1388 n.4 (8th Cir. 1995); Pratt v. Rowland, 65 F.3d 802, 806–07 (9th Cir. 1995). In *Young v. Harper*, 117 S. Ct. 1148, 1150 (1997), a unanimous Court held that Oklahoma's Preparole Conditional Supervision Program, "a program employed by the State of Oklahoma to reduce the overcrowding of its prisons[,] was sufficiently like parole that a person in the program was entitled to the procedural protections set forth in *Morrissey v. Brewer*, 408 U.S. 471 . . . (1972), before he could be removed from it."

constitutionally adequate.[68] The issue of what procedural safeguards must accompany a state's deprivation of a constitutionally protected interest is a matter of federal law.[69]

In *Mathews v. Eldridge*,[70] the Court set forth three competing factors to be weighed in determining the sufficiency of procedural safeguards accompanying deprivations caused by the state:

> First, the private interest that will be affected by the official action; second, the risk of an erroneous deprivation of such interest through the procedures used, and the probable value, if any, of additional or substitute procedural safeguards; and, finally, the Government's interest, including the function involved and the fiscal and administrative burdens that the additional or substitute procedural requirement would entail.[71]

Generally, due process requires some notice and an opportunity to be heard prior to the deprivation of a protected interest.[72] In certain cases, however, a post-deprivation remedy is adequate. For example, a state does not violate the due process clause of the Fourteenth Amendment by failing to provide notice and a hearing before suspending without pay a university police officer who had been arrested and charged with drug possession. The arrest and the filing of the charges by a third party, and the employer's need to dismiss employees in a position of "great public trust," strongly weigh against granting a predeprivation hearing.[73]

Another type of due process claim arises when a plaintiff has been deprived of life, liberty, or property by state officials acting pursuant to established state procedure that failed to provide for predeprivation process in a situation where such process was possible, practicable, and constitu-

---

68. Zinermon v. Burch, 494 U.S. 113, 126 (1990).

69. Vitek v. Jones, 445 U.S. 480, 491 (1980).

70. 424 U.S. 319 (1976).

71. *Id.* at 335. *See, e.g., Washington v. Harper*, 494 U.S. 210 (1990), where a mentally ill state prisoner challenged the prison's administration of antipsychotic drugs to him against his will without a judicial hearing to determine the appropriateness of such treatment. The prison policy required the treatment decision to be made by a hearing committee consisting of a psychiatrist, psychologist, and the prison facility's associate superintendent. The Court applied the *Mathews* balancing test and found the established procedure constitutionally sufficient. *Id.* at 229–33.

72. Cleveland Bd. of Educ. v. Loudermill, 470 U.S. 532, 542 (1985).

73. Gilbert v. Homar, 117 S. Ct. 1807, 1813 (1997).

tionally required.[74] The erroneous deprivation must have been foreseeable; the predeprivation process practicable; and the challenged conduct "authorized."[75]

In contrast, under the *Parratt/Hudson* doctrine,[76] there is no procedural due process claim where the deprivation was unforeseeable, random, unauthorized, and where the state provided an adequate post-deprivation remedy.[77] This doctrine represents a "special case of the general *Mathews v. Eldridge* analysis, in which postdeprivation tort remedies are all the process that is due, simply because they are the only remedies that the state could be expected to provide."[78] In short, the value of a predeprivation procedural safeguard for unforeseeable conduct is "negligible" in preventing the deprivation.[79]

In addition to these two types of procedural due process claims is the Court's fact-specific analysis in *Zinermon v. Burch*.[80] In *Zinermon* the plaintiff, Darrell Burch, was admitted to a state mental hospital as a "voluntary" patient under circumstances that clearly indicated he was incapable of informed consent. Burch alleged that his five-month hospitalization deprived him of liberty without due process of law.

In holding that Burch's complaint was sufficient to state a procedural due process claim, the Court stated: "Burch's suit is neither an action

---

74. Logan v. Zimmerman Brush Co., 455 U.S. 422, 435–36 (1982).

75. Zinermon v. Burch, 494 U.S. 113, 136 (1990).

76. Hudson v. Palmer, 468 U.S. 517, 531–33 (1984); Parratt v. Taylor, 451 U.S. 527, 543 (1981), *overruled in part*, Daniels v. Williams, 474 U.S. 327 (1986). In *Daniels*, the Court overruled *Parratt* to the extent that the case had held that a deprivation within the meaning of the Fourteenth Amendment due process clause could be effected by mere negligent conduct. *Id.* at 330–31.

77. *Compare, e.g.*, Brown v. Hot, Sexy & Safer Prods., Inc., 68 F.3d 525, 536–37 (1st Cir. 1995) (concluding that officials' failure to adhere to sex education policy was "random and unauthorized" within meaning of *Parratt/Hudson* doctrine), *cert. denied*, 116 S. Ct. 1044 (1966), *with* Alexander v. Ieyoub, 62 F.3d 709, 712 (5th Cir. 1995) (finding that defendants' conduct—delaying forfeiture proceeding for nearly three years—was authorized under state law where defendants had discretion to institute proceedings whenever they wanted).

78. Zinermon v. Burch, 494 U.S. 113, 128 (1990).

79. *Id.* at 129.

80. 494 U.S. 113 (1990). *Zinermon* has been interpreted as creating a category of procedural due process claims that falls outside "two clearly delineated categories: those involving a direct challenge to an established state procedure or those challenging random and unauthorized acts." Mertik v. Blalock, 983 F.2d 1353, 1365 (6th Cir. 1993).

challenging the facial adequacy of a State's statutory procedures, nor an action based only on state officials' random and unauthorized violation of state laws. Burch is not simply attempting to blame the State for misconduct by its employees. He seeks to hold state officials accountable for their abuse of their broadly delegated, uncircumscribed power to effect the deprivation at issue."[81]

Substantive Due Process Claims

The protections afforded by the substantive component of the due process clause have generally been limited to "matters relating to marriage, family, procreation, and the right to bodily integrity."[82] Noting that "the guideposts for responsible decisionmaking in this unchartered area are scarce and open-ended[,]"[83] the Supreme Court has in recent years expressed a reluctance to expand the scope of substantive due process protection.[84] Whenever "an explicit textual source of constitutional protection" addresses particular behavior, courts must rely on the more explicit source of protection to analyze the claim, rather than the amorphous and open-ended concept of substantive due process.[85] For example, substantive due process protects individuals who have been subjected to excessive force in a nonseizure, nonprisoner context because neither the Fourth nor Eighth Amendment applies.[86]

81. *Zinermon*, 494 U.S. at 136.

82. Albright v. Oliver, 510 U.S. 266, 272 (1994) (plurality opinion).

83. *Id.*

84. *See* Washington v. Glucksberg, 117 S. Ct. 2258, 2267 (1997); Albright v. Oliver, 510 U.S. 266, 271(1994); Collins v. City of Harker Heights, 503 U.S. 115, 125 (1992). *But see* BMW of N. Am., Inc. v. Gore, 116 S. Ct. 1589 (1996) (holding due process clause prohibits state from imposing "grossly excessive" punishment on tortfeasor).

85. *Albright*, 510 U.S. at 273 (citing Graham v. Connor, 490 U.S. 386, 395 (1989)); *accord* County of Sacramento v. Lewis, 523 U.S. —, 118 S. Ct. 1708, 1715 (1998).

86. *See* County of Sacramento v. Lewis, 523 U.S. —, 118 S. Ct. 1708, 1715 (1998) (stating that "[s]ubstantive due process analysis is therefore inappropriate . . . only if [the] claim is 'covered by' the Fourth Amendment") (discussed *infra* text accompanying notes 106–12, 153–57).

In *United States v. Lanier*, 117 S. Ct. 1219 (1997), the Supreme Court, in dicta, previously endorsed this view, noting that:

Graham v. Connor . . . does not hold that all constitutional claims relating to physically abusive government conduct must arise under either the Fourth or Eighth Amendments; rather, *Graham* simply requires that if a constitutional claim is covered by a specific constitutional provision, such as the Fourth or Eighth Amendment, the claim must be analyzed under the standard appropriate to that specific provision, not under the ru-

DeShaney and Affirmative Duty Cases

In *DeShaney v. Winnebago County Department of Social Services*,[87] a majority of the Supreme Court held that nothing in the due process clause
of the Fourteenth Amendment creates an affirmative duty on the part of
the state to "protect the life, liberty, and property of its citizens against
invasion by private actors."[88] The Court concluded that "[a]s a general
matter . . . a State's failure to protect an individual against private violence simply does not constitute a violation of the Due Process Clause."[89]

In contrast, *DeShaney* also recognized an affirmative "duty to protect"
when the state incarcerates or involuntarily institutionalizes a person.[90]
Plaintiffs who have successfully survived the *DeShaney* analysis, outside
the strict confines of incarceration or involuntary institutionalization,
have asserted substantive due process claims arising in one of two contexts: (1) the plaintiff was in the "functional custody" of the state when
harmed, or (2) the state created or increased the danger to which the
plaintiff was exposed.

Functional Custody

Where the affirmative duty is grounded in the concept of "custody," a
number of courts have taken the position that the plaintiff must have
been *involuntarily* in the state's custody when harmed.[91] In *DeShaney*, the

bric of substantive due process.
Id. at 1228 n.7.

87. 489 U.S. 189 (1989). Many readers are no doubt familiar with the tragic facts of
DeShaney. A four-year-old boy had been repeatedly beaten by his father. The county
child-protection agency had monitored Joshua's case through social workers, but failed to
protect him from his father's last beating, which left the child permanently brain dam-
aged. *Id.* at 192–93.

88. *Id.* at 195.

89. *Id.* at 197.

90. *See, e.g.,* Youngberg v. Romeo, 457 U.S. 307 (1982) (substantive due process component of Fourteenth Amendment due process clause imposes duty on state to provide
for safety and medical needs of involuntarily committed mental patients); Estelle v. Gamble, 429 U.S. 97 (1976) (state has constitutional duty to provide adequate medical care to
incarcerated prisoners).

91. *See, e.g., Walton v. Alexander*, 44 F.3d 1297, 1304 (5th Cir. 1995) (en banc), where
the court notes:

> Recurring throughout [the] cases that we have decided since *DeShaney* is the iteration of
> the principle that if the person claiming the right of state protection is voluntarily within
> the care or custody of a state agency, he has no substantive due process right to the
> state's protection from harm inflicted by third party nonstate actors. We thus conclude

Court acknowledged that the situation where the state removes a child from "free society" and places him or her in a foster home might be "sufficiently analogous to incarceration or institutionalization to give rise to an affirmative duty to protect."[92] The lower federal courts that have ruled on the issue since *DeShaney* have uniformly recognized a constitutional right to protection from unnecessary harm on the part of foster children involuntarily placed by the state in a foster care situation.[93]

The majority of courts have rejected arguments that public school-children, by virtue of compulsory attendance laws, are in the "functional custody" of the state during school hours.[94] These courts have held that

that *DeShaney* stands for the proposition that the state creates a "special relationship" with a person only when the person is involuntarily taken into state custody and held against his will through the affirmative power of the state; otherwise, the state has no duty arising under the Constitution to protect its citizens against harm by private actors.

At least one circuit has suggested that the concept of "in custody" for *DeShaney* purposes of triggering an affirmative duty to protect entails more than a "simple criminal arrest." *See* Estate of Stevens v. City of Green Bay, 105 F.3d 1169, 1175 (7th Cir. 1997) ("The Supreme Court's express rationale in *DeShaney* for recognizing a constitutional duty does not match the circumstances of a simple criminal arrest. . . . This rationale on its face requires more than a person riding in the back seat of an unlocked police car for a few minutes.").

92. *DeShaney*, 489 U.S. at 201 n.9.

93. *See, e.g.,* Camp v. Gregory, 67 F.3d 1286, 1297 (7th Cir. 1995) (noting that "when a DCFS caseworker places a child in a home knowing that his caretaker cannot provide reasonable supervision, and the failure to provide that degree of supervision and care results in injury to the child outside of the home, it might be appropriate, depending upon the facts culminating in the injury, for the caseworker to be held liable for a deprivation of liberty"); Norfleet v. Arkansas Dep't of Human Servs., 989 F.2d 289, 293 (8th Cir. 1993) (recognizing that "[c]ases from this and other circuits clearly demonstrate that imprisonment is not the only custodial relationship in which the state must safeguard an individual's civil rights"). *But see* D.W. v. Rogers, 113 F.3d 1214, 1218 (11th Cir. 1997) (holding "that the state's affirmative obligation to render services to an individual depends not on whether the state has legal custody of that person, but on whether the state has physically confined or restrained the person"); White v. Chambliss, 112 F.3d 731, 737 (4th Cir. 1997) ("Given the state of this circuit's law on the issue and the absence of controlling Supreme Court authority, we cannot say that a right to affirmative state protection for children placed in foster care was clearly established at the time of Keena's death."); Wooten v. Campbell, 49 F.3d 696, 699–701 (11th Cir. 1995) (finding no "substantive due process right is implicated where a public agency is awarded legal custody of a child, but does not control that child's physical custody except to arrange court-ordered visitation with the non-custodial parent").

94. *See, e.g.,* Doe v. Hillsboro Indep. Sch. Dist., 113 F.3d 1412, 1415 (5th Cir. 1997) (en banc) (joining "every circuit court that has considered the issue in holding that com-

the state does not have a duty to protect students from harm inflicted by fellow students or other private actors.[95] Courts have likewise rejected the notion that individuals in public housing[96] or employees of a public entity[97] are in the "functional custody" of the state and thus owed an af-

pulsory school attendance . . . does not create the custodial relationship envisioned by *DeShaney*"); Doe v. Claiborne County, 103 F.3d 495, 510 (6th Cir. 1996) (holding that school's "in loco parentis status or a state's compulsory attendance laws do not sufficiently 'restrain' students to raise a school's common-law obligation to the rank of a constitutional duty"); Nabozny v. Podlesny, 92 F.3d 458–59 (7th Cir. 1996) (concluding that "local school administrations have no affirmative constitutional duty to protect students from the private actions of third parties while they attend school"); Walton v. Alexander, 44 F.3d 1297, 1305 (5th Cir. 1995) (en banc) (holding that, where attendance at school was voluntary and there was a right to leave at will, child's "status as a resident student [did not place] him within the narrow class of persons . . . entitled to claim from the state a constitutional duty of protection from harm at the hands of private parties"); Wright v. Lovin, 32 F.3d 538, 540 (11th Cir. 1994) (stating that "To date, every federal circuit court of appeal to address the question of whether compulsory school attendance laws create the necessary custodial relationship between school and student to give rise to a constitutional duty to protect students from harm by nonstate actors has rejected the existence of any such duty." (citing cases)).

It is worth noting the following dicta in Justice Scalia's opinion in *Vernonia School District 47Jv. Acton*, 515 U.S. 646, 655 (1995):

> While we do not, of course, suggest that public schools as a general matter have such a degree of control over children as to give rise to a constitutional "duty to protect," see *DeShaney* . . . [cite omitted], we have acknowledged that for many purposes "school authorities ac[t] *in loco parentis*," [cite omitted], with the power and indeed the duty to "inculcate the habits and manners of civility," [cite omitted].

95. Schoolchildren have a liberty interest in their bodily integrity that is protected by the due process clause against deprivation by the state. Ingraham v. Wright, 430 U.S. 651, 673–74 (1977). Therefore, *DeShaney* does not apply where the alleged harm is attributed to a state actor, generally a teacher or other school official. *See, e.g.,* Stoneking v. Bradford Area Sch. Dist., 882 F.2d 720, 724 (3d Cir. 1989) (*Stoneking II*) (opinion on remand) (recognizing that the situation in that case was very different from *DeShaney* because the injury—sexual molestation—resulted from the conduct of a state employee, not a private actor), *cert. denied*, 493 U.S. 1044 (1990).

96. *See, e.g.,* Dawson v. Milwaukee, 930 F.2d 1283, 1285 (7th Cir. 1991) (presence in publicly subsidized housing is not functional equivalent of being "in custody").

97. *See, e.g.,* Wallace v. Adkins, 115 F.3d 427, 429 (7th Cir. 1997) ("[P]rison guards ordered to stay at their posts are not in the kind of custodial setting required to create a special relationship for 14th Amendment substantive due process purposes."); Liebson v. New Mexico Corrections Dep't, 73 F.3d 274, 276 (10th Cir. 1996) (librarian assigned to provide library services to inmates housed in maximum security unit of the New Mexico State Penitentiary was not in state's custody or held against her will; employment relationship was "completely voluntary"); Lewellen v. Metropolitan Gov't of Nashville, 34 F.3d

firmative duty of protection. In *Collins v. City of Harker Heights*,[98] the Supreme Court unanimously affirmed the view that "the Due Process Clause does not impose an independent federal obligation upon municipalities to provide certain minimal levels of safety and security in the workplace. . . ."[99]

State-Created Danger

In concluding that the state had not deprived Joshua DeShaney of any constitutionally protected rights, the Supreme Court suggested that the result might have been different if the state had played a role in creating the dangers to which Joshua was exposed or had increased his vulnerability to these dangers.[100] While *DeShaney* makes clear that the state's mere awareness of a risk of harm to an individual will not suffice to impose an affirmative duty to provide protection,[101] if the state creates the danger confronting the individual, it may then have a corresponding duty to protect.[102] Moreover, the Supreme Court's decision in *Collins v.*

---

345 (6th Cir. 1994) (workman accidentally injured on school construction project has no substantive due process claim), *cert. denied*, 115 S. Ct. 963 (1995).

98. 503 U.S. 115 (1992).

99. *Id.* at 130.

100. DeShaney v. Winnebago County Dep't of Soc. Servs., 489 U.S. 189, 201 (1989).

101. *Id.* at 200 ("The affirmative duty to protect arises not from the State's knowledge of the individual's predicament or from its expressions of intent to help him . . . ."). *See also* Pinder v. Johnson, 54 F.3d 1169, 1175 (4th Cir. 1995) (en banc) ("By requiring a custodial context as the condition for an affirmative duty, *DeShaney* rejected the idea that such a duty can arise solely from an official's awareness of a specific risk or from promises of aid.").

102. *See, e.g.,* Estate of Stevens v. City of Green Bay, 105 F.3d 1169, 1177 (7th Cir. 1997) ("To recover under this [state-created danger] theory, the estate must demonstrate that the state greatly increased the danger to Stevens while constricting access to self-help; it must cut off all avenues of aid without providing a reasonable alternative. Only then may a constitutional injury have occurred."); Seamons v. Snow, 84 F.3d 1226 (10th Cir. 1996) (noting that "[i]n addition to the 'special relationship' doctrine, we have held that state officials can be liable for the acts of third parties where those officials 'created the danger' that caused the harm"); Pinder v. Johnson, 54 F.3d 1169, 1177 (4th Cir. 1995) (en banc) (observing that "[w]hen the state itself creates the dangerous situation that resulted in a victim's injury, the absence of a custodial relationship may not be dispositive"); Reed v. Gardner, 986 F.2d 1122, 1126–27 (7th Cir. 1993) (holding that "plaintiffs . . . may state claims for civil rights violations if they allege state action that creates, or substantially contributes to the creation of, a danger or renders citizens more vulnerable to a danger than they otherwise would have been. . ."); Dwares v. City of New York, 985 F.2d 94, 99

City of Harker Heights,[103] holding that there is no substantive due process right to a safe work environment,[104] has not precluded the imposition of constitutional liability on state officials who deliberately or intentionally place public employees in a dangerous situation without adequate protection.[105]

(2d Cir. 1993) (finding *DeShaney* not controlling where plaintiff alleged that defendant-officers had made demonstrators more vulnerable to assaults); Freeman v. Ferguson, 911 F.2d 52, 55 (8th Cir. 1990) (noting "[*DeShaney*] analysis establishes the possibility that a constitutional duty to protect an individual against private violence may exist in a non-custodial setting if the state has taken affirmative action which increases the individual's danger of or vulnerability to, such violence beyond the level it would have been at absent state action"); Wood v. Ostrander, 879 F.2d 583, 590 (9th Cir. 1989) (concluding an affirmative duty to protect was owed plaintiff by a police officer who arrested the driver of the car in which plaintiff was a passenger, impounded the vehicle, and left plaintiff stranded in a high-crime area at 2:30 a.m., resulting in rape of plaintiff), *cert. denied*, 498 U.S. 938 (1990). *Compare* Kneipp v. Tedder, 95 F.3d 1199, 1201, 1209 n.22 (3d Cir. 1996) (adopting the 'state-created danger' theory as a "viable mechanism for establishing a constitutional violation under 42 U.S.C. § 1983," where severely inebriated woman was stopped by police and then allowed to proceed home alone. "[T]he relationship requirement . . . contemplates some contact such that the plaintiff was a foreseeable victim of a defendant's acts in a tort sense"), *with* Bogle v. City of Warner Robins, 953 F. Supp. 1563, 1570 (M.D. Ga. 1997) (holding that "plaintiff was not deprived of her constitutional rights under the Fourteenth Amendment when police officers released her from custody in an impaired state" and plaintiff was subsequently raped by a third party).

103. 503 U.S. 115 (1992).

104. *Id.* at 130.

105. *See, e.g.,* L.W. v. Grubbs (*L.W. I*), 974 F.2d 119, 120–21 (9th Cir. 1992) (concluding that plaintiff, a registered nurse, stated a constitutional claim against defendant correctional officers, where defendants knew inmate was a violent sex offender, likely to assault plaintiff if alone with her, yet defendants intentionally assigned inmate to work alone with plaintiff in clinic), *cert. denied*, 113 S. Ct. 2442 (1993); Cornelius v. Town of Highland Lake, 880 F.2d 348, 359 (11th Cir. 1989) (holding that where the defendants had put the plaintiff, a town clerk, in a "unique position of danger" by causing inmates who were inadequately supervised to be present in the town hall, then "under the special danger approach as well as the special relationship approach . . . the defendants owed [the plaintiff] a duty to protect her from the harm they created"), *cert. denied*, 494 U.S. 1066 (1990). *But see* Mitchell v. Duval County Sch. Bd., 107 F.3d 837, 839 n.3 (11th Cir. 1997) (per curiam) (noting that "*Cornelius* may not have survived *Collins v. City of Harker Heights*, 503 U.S. 115 . . . (1992), where the Supreme Court held that a voluntary employment relationship does not impose a constitutional duty on government employers to provide a reasonably safe work environment"—but holding that even if *Cornelius* has not been undermined, the plaintiff did not make out a state-created danger claim where "the school neither placed Mitchell in a dangerous location nor placed the assailants in the

State of Mind

The substantive due process component of the Fourteenth Amendment protects against "arbitrary action."[106] For an action to be arbitrary it must "shock the conscience";[107] negligent action is clearly insufficient to establish a violation of substantive due process.[108] In *County of Sacramento v. Lewis*,[109] the Court explained that determining shocking conduct depends on the type of substantive due process claim asserted. For example, when prison officials are deliberately indifferent to a pretrial detainee's serious medical needs, their actions "shock the conscience";[110] but when police officers engage in a high-speed pursuit that results in the death of one of the suspected offenders, their actions are shocking only if they acted with malice, that is, with "intent to harm the suspects physically or to worsen their legal plight."[111] Thus, a police officer's deliberate indifference to the risks arising from a high-speed pursuit is insufficient to establish individual liability.

Two factors aid courts in considering whether conduct is shocking: whether there was time for reflection and whether there were competing governmental needs:

> [L]iability for deliberate indifference to inmate [medical] welfare rests upon the luxury enjoyed by prison officials of having time to make un-hurried judgments, upon the chance for repeated reflection, largely un-

---

place where Mitchell was." *Id.* at 840.).

106. County of Sacramento v. Lewis, 523 U.S. —, 118 S. Ct. 1708, 1716 (1998); *see also* Collins v. City of Harker Heights, 503 U.S. 115, 130 (1992) (holding that city's alleged failure to train or warn sanitation department employees was not arbitrary).

107. *County of Sacramento*, 118 S. Ct. at 1717. Justice Souter authored an opinion joined by five Justices: Chief Justice Rehnquist and Justices O'Connor, Kennedy, Ginsburg, and Breyer. He stated that when a plaintiff challenges a "specific act of a governmental officer," rather than legislation, *id.* at 1716, the plaintiff must show that the act "shocks the conscience" to establish a substantive due process violation. *Id.* at 1717. Justices Kennedy and O'Connor, however, in a concurring opinion, stated that "the reasons the Court gives in support of its judgment go far toward establishing that objective considerations, including history and precedent, are the controlling principle, regardless of whether the State's action is legislative or executive in character." *Id.* at 1722 (Kennedy, J., concurring).

108. Davidson v. Cannon, 474 U.S. 344, 347 (1986); Daniels v. Williams, 474 U.S. 327, 333 (1986).

109. 523 U.S. —, 118 S. Ct. 1708 (1998).

110. *Id.* at 1718 (citing Estelle v. Gamble, 429 U.S. 97, 104 (1976)).

111. *Id.* at 1720.

complicated by the pulls of competing obligations. When such extended opportunities to do better are teamed with protracted failure
even to care, indifference is truly shocking. But when unforeseen circumstances demand an officer's instant judgment, even precipitate
recklessness fails to inch close enough to harmful purpose to spark the
shock that implicates [the substantive component of the Fourteenth
Amendment].[112]

In the context of a high-speed pursuit, officers must act quickly to weigh
the competing concerns of effective law enforcement against the risks of a
pursuit. Liability attaches only when officers act maliciously.

Many courts apply a "professional judgment" standard to substantive
due process claims raised by involuntarily placed foster children.[113] The
Supreme Court articulated this standard in *Youngberg v. Romeo*,[114]
holding that state officials who commit someone involuntarily (a mentally handicapped patient) are liable only if their decision was "such a
substantial departure from accepted professional judgment, practice, or
standards as to demonstrate that the person responsible actually did not
base the decision on such judgment."[115]

Use of Force by Governmental Officials

Governmental officials may be subject to § 1983 lawsuits when they use
force to control suspects, pretrial detainees, and prisoners. The source of
the right for claims against these officials depends on the plaintiff's status
at the time officials used force: the Fourth Amendment[116] applies to
"seized" individuals and prohibits the use of unreasonable force;[117] and
the Eighth Amendment[118] applies to prisoners and prohibits cruel and

---

112. *Id.*

113. *See, e.g.,* Yvonne L. v. New Mexico Dep't of Human Servs., 959 F.2d 883, 893–94
(10th Cir. 1992) (adopting professional judgment standard, rather than deliberate indifference, in foster care setting).

114. 457 U.S. 307 (1982).

115. *Id.* at 323.

116. U.S. Const. amend. VIII (stating "cruel and unusual punishments [shall not be]
inflicted").

117. Graham v. Connor, 490 U.S. 386, 394–95 (1989); *accord* County of Sacramento
v. Lewis, 523 U.S. —, 118 S. Ct. 1708, 1715 (1998).

118. U.S. Const. amend. IV (stating "[the] right of the people to be secure in their
persons . . . against unreasonable . . . seizures . . . .").

unusual punishment.[119] Because the Fourth and Eighth Amendment rights have been incorporated by the due process clause of the Fourteenth Amendment, state officials are subject to § 1983 lawsuits under these amendments. The Supreme Court has described the standard for measuring force under the Fourth and Eighth Amendments.[120]

Under the substantive due process component of the Fourteenth Amendment, use-of-force claims are actionable if they constitute a deprivation of "liberty . . . without due process of law."[121] A substantive due process claim challenging the use of force may lie only if neither the Fourth [122] nor the Eighth Amendment applies. For example, if the use of force constituted a "seizure" within the meaning of the Fourth Amendment, the claim arises only under the Fourth Amendment as incorporated by the due process clause.[123] In contrast, if officers engage in a high-speed pursuit and do *not* "seize" an injured person, the Fourth Amendment would not apply, and the use-of-force claim may be actionable only under the substantive due process component of the Fourteenth Amendment.[124]

Although the "Due Process Clause protects a pretrial detainee from use of force that amounts to punishment,"[125] it is unclear if a plaintiff can be both a pretrial detainee and a suspect "seized" within the meaning of the Fourth Amendment. The Supreme Court has stated, "Our decisions have not resolved the question whether the Fourth Amendment continues to provide individuals with protection against deliberate use of excessive force beyond the point at which arrest ends and pretrial detention begins."[126] As a result, some lower courts question whether the Fourth Amendment applies to force claims asserted by pretrial detainees.[127]

---

119. Hudson v. McMillian, 112 S. Ct. 995, 999 (1992); Whitley v. Albers, 475 U.S. 312, 321 (1986).

120. *See infra* text accompanying notes 130 & 152–57.

121. U.S. Const. amend. XIV, § 1 (stating "[n]o state shall . . . deprive any person of life, liberty . . . without due process of law . . . .").

122. *County of Sacramento*, 118 S. Ct. at 1715. *See also* United States v. Lanier, 117 S. Ct. 1219, 1228 n.7 (1997); Albright v. Oliver, 510 U.S. 266, 273 (1994) (plurality opinion); Graham v. Connor, 490 U.S. 386, 395 (1989).

123. *Graham*, 490 U.S. at 395.

124. *County of Sacramento*, 118 S. Ct. at 1715.

125. *Graham*, 490 U.S. at 395 n.10.

126. *Id.*

127. *See, e.g.*, Riley v. Dorton, 115 F.3d 1159, 1163–64 (4th Cir. 1997) (detailing the

Unreasonable Force Claims Under the Fourth Amendment

Whether police officers have violated the Fourth Amendment during an investigation or arrest depends upon the resolution of two issues: (1) In using force, did officials "seize" the suspect within the meaning of the Fourth Amendment?[128] and (2) Was the force objectively unreasonable?[129] If officers both seized the plaintiff and used objectively unreasonable force, then the plaintiff has stated a claim under the Fourth Amendment. If no seizure occurred, then the use of force is not actionable under the Fourth Amendment; the force, however, might be actionable under the Fourteenth Amendment.[130] Resolving these two issues requires scrutiny of the Supreme Court's definition of a "seizure" and of "objectively unreasonable" force.

The Supreme Court has articulated the following three definitions for determining when officers have seized an individual:

1. Whether "the officer, by means of physical force or show of authority, has in some way restrained the liberty of a citizen."[131]

2. Whether a "reasonable person would have believed that he was not free to leave" and the person in fact submitted to the assertion of authority.[132]

3. Whether there was "a governmental termination of freedom of movement through means intentionally applied."[133]

---

conflict in the circuits: "The Second, Sixth, and Ninth Circuits do extend Fourth Amendment coverage to the period the suspect remains with the arresting officers . . . . In sum, we agree with the Fifth, Seventh, and Eleventh Circuits that the Fourth Amendment does not embrace a theory of 'continuing seizure' and does not extend to the alleged mistreatment of arrestees or pretrial detainees in custody"); *see generally* Albright v. Oliver, 510 U.S. 266, 279 (1994) (Ginsburg, J., concurring) (stating that a person had been "seized" within meaning of Fourth Amendment by his arrest and conditional release after posting bail).

128. *Graham*, 490 U.S. at 395–96.

129. *Id.*

130. *See generally* County of Sacramento v. Lewis, 523 U.S. —, 118 S. Ct. 1708, 1715 (1998) (stating that if a police officer's use of force during a high-speed pursuit did not result in a seizure, substantive due process analysis is appropriate).

131. Terry v. Ohio, 392 U.S. 1, 19 n.16 (1968).

132. California v. Hodari D., 499 U.S. 621, 628 (1991); *see also* United States v. Mendenhall, 446 U.S. 544, 554 (1980) (opinion for Justices Stewart and Rehnquist); I.N.S. v. Delgado, 466 U.S. 210, 215 (1984).

These definitions focus on the assertion of authority and the use of physical force. When officers use physical force, the first and third definitions of seizure are applicable. The first definition simply states that the use of physical force can effectuate a seizure; the third definition, articulated twenty-one years later, requires that the application of force be "intentional." Thus, if a police officer accidentally hits someone with his vehicle, the officer used physical force, but no seizure occurred because the force was not intentional.[134]

Determining whether officers used unreasonable force when they seized a suspect is a fact-specific inquiry using the Fourth Amendment standard of reasonableness. Two Supreme Court decisions assessed the reasonableness of different types of force.

In *Tennessee v. Garner*,[135] the Court held that the use of deadly force was objectively unreasonable.[136] A police officer, who had reason to believe that a suspect had just burglarized a home, commanded the fleeing suspect to stop. When the suspect did not stop, the police officer shot and killed him. Under these circumstances, the shooting was not justified under the standard articulated by the Court: "[I]f the suspect threatens the officer with a weapon or there is probable cause to believe that he has committed a crime involving the infliction or threatened infliction of serious physical harm, deadly force may be used if necessary to prevent es-

---

133. Brower v. County of Inyo, 489 U.S. 593, 597 (1989) (use of roadblock to stop fleeing motorist constituted seizure; whether the act was intentional is an objective inquiry—the question is whether a reasonable officer would have believed that the means used would have caused the suspect to stop).

134. *County of Sacramento*, 118 S. Ct. at 1715 (stating that no seizure occurred when officer accidentally hit passenger of pursued motorcyclist).

Most excessive force claims under the Fourth Amendment involve the infliction of physical injury. Also actionable are claims involving psychological injury. *See, e.g.,* McDonald v. Haskins, 966 F.2d 292 (7th Cir. 1992) (holding that a nine-year-old child stated an unreasonable force claim under the Fourth Amendment by alleging that an officer held a gun to his head while executing a search warrant, even though he posed no threat to the officer and did not attempt to flee); *see generally* Hudson v. McMillian, 112 S. Ct. 995, 1004 (1992) (Blackmun, J., concurring) (psychological harm can constitute "cruel and unusual punishment under the Eighth Amendment") (citing Wisniewski v. Kennard, 901 F.2d 1276, 1277 (5th Cir.) (placing gun in prisoner's mouth and threatening to shoot stated a claim under the Eighth Amendment), *cert. denied*, 111 S. Ct. 309 (1990)).

135. 471 U.S. 1 (1985).

136. *Id.* at 11–12.

cape, and if, where feasible, some warning has been given."[137] In short, the suspect posed no danger to the officer or the community (burglary does not involve the infliction of "serious physical harm").[138]

Assessing danger is also important in evaluating the use of nondeadly force. In *Graham v. Connor*,[139] the Supreme Court held that three factors were relevant in determining the reasonableness of force: (1) "the severity of the crime at issue"; (2) "whether the suspect poses an immediate threat to the safety of the officers or others"; and (3) "whether he is actively resisting arrest or attempting to evade arrest by flight."[140] In articulating these factors, the Court did not state that these were the only factors relevant to the reasonableness inquiry. Reasonableness requires a balancing of interests, evaluating the circumstances present at the time the officers act, and allowing the officers some deference because they often have to make "split-second judgments."[141] This reasonableness inquiry is an objective one. Plaintiffs do not have to prove that officers acted in bad faith;[142] such evidence, however, would be admissible to challenge the officers' credibility.[143]

Malicious Force Claims Under the Eighth Amendment

Although malice is not an element of a Fourth Amendment claim, it is the central inquiry under the Eighth Amendment for a claim alleging the use of excessive force. The Eighth Amendment standard is "whether force was applied in a good-faith effort to maintain or restore discipline, or maliciously and sadistically to cause harm."[144] In two decisions, the Supreme Court held that this standard applies to the use of force to control prisoners, whether to diffuse a riot[145] or to impose discipline.[146]

---

137. *Id.*
138. *Id.* at 11.
139. 490 U.S. 386 (1989).
140. *Id.* at 396.
141. *Id.* at 397.
142. *Id.*
143. *Id.* at 399 n.12.
144. Hudson v. McMillian, 112 S. Ct. 995, 999 (1992); Whitley v. Albers, 475 U.S. 312, 321 (1986).
145. *Whitley*, 475 U.S. at 321.
146. *Hudson*, 112 S. Ct. at 999.

In *Whitley v. Albers*,[147] the Supreme Court held that five factors were relevant in determining whether officers acted maliciously when they used force to quell a prison riot: (1) the need for force; (2) "the relationship between the need and the amount of force that was used"; (3) "the extent of injury inflicted"; (4) "the extent of the threat to the safety of staff and inmates"; and (5) "any efforts made to temper the severity of a forceful response."[148] In articulating the standard, the Court also expressed a need to defer to the judgment of prison officials.

The Court later applied this standard in *Hudson v. McMillian*,[149] where officials did not face the exigencies of a prison riot. The Court interpreted the third factor as not requiring a "significant" injury.[150] However, plaintiffs need to allege something more than a *de minimus* injury unless the force used was "repugnant to the conscience of mankind." [151] The extent of an injury thus became just one factor in determining whether officials acted with malice.

Thus, the Supreme Court has clearly articulated factors for determining malice under the Eighth Amendment and unreasonable force under the Fourth Amendment. It has not done so, however, for Fourteenth Amendment force claims.

Excessive Force Claims Under the Fourteenth Amendment

Although the Supreme Court has not elaborated on the standard for use-of-force claims under the Fourteenth Amendment, it has stated that "the Due Process Clause protects a pretrial detainee from the use of excessive force that amounts to punishment."[152]

More recently, the Court held in *County of Sacramento v. Lewis*[153] that to violate the substantive due process component of the Fourteenth Amendment, an official's actions must "shock the conscience." [154] Officials commit shocking actions when they use force with the intent to

147. 475 U.S. 312 (1986).

148. *Id*. at 321.

149. 112 S. Ct. 995, 999 (1992).

150. *Id.* at 1000.

151. *Id.* (quoting *Whitley*, 475 U.S. at 327 (quoting Estelle v. Gamble, 429 U.S. 97, 104 (1976))).

152. Graham v. Connor, 490 U.S. 386, 395 n.10 (1989).

153. 523 U.S. —, 118 S. Ct. 1708 (1998).

154. *Id*. at 1717 (citing Rochin v. California, 342 U.S. 165, 172–73 (1952)).

harm a person.[155] The Court derived this malice standard by likening a police officer's actions during a high-speed pursuit to a prison guard's actions during a riot:[156] both must act quickly with little time for reflection.

Although the Court did not state that the malice standard applies to force claims raised by pretrial detainees, at least one lower court prior to *County of Sacramento* had determined that malice was the appropriate standard.[157]

Malicious Prosecution Claims Under the Fourth Amendment

Determining whether plaintiffs have alleged a malicious prosecution claim under the Fourth Amendment is difficult because the standard for evaluating these claims is unclear after the Supreme Court's decisions in *Heck v. Humphrey*[158] and *Albright v. Oliver.*[159] In these decisions, the Court merely declared what is *not* a malicious prosecution claim.

Prior to these decisions, many lower courts used the commo n-law elements of a malicious prosecution tort to establish a constitutional violation of substantive due process.[160] The common-law elements included (1) institution of a criminal proceeding; (2) without probable cause; (3) with malice; and (4) termination in favor of the criminal defendant.[161] In *Albright*, the Court held that substantive due process was *not* the basis for a constitutional claim of malicious prosecution. Such a claim *may* arise under the Fourth Amendment. In *Heck*, the Court held

---

155. *Id.* at 1711.

156. *Id.* at 1720.

157. *See, e.g.,* Valencia v. Wiggins, 981 F.2d 1440 (5th Cir.), *cert. denied,* 113 S. Ct. 2998 (1993); *but see generally* Sandin v. Conner, 115 S. Ct. 2293, 2300 (1995) (distinguishing claims raised by prisoners from claims raised by detainees: "The punishment of incarcerated prisoners . . . serves different aims than those found invalid [for pretrial detainees]. . . . It effectuates prison management and prisoner rehabilitative goals.").

158. 114 S. Ct. 2364, 2372 (1994). For a thorough treatment of the relationship between habeas corpus relief and § 1983 relief, see Ira Robbins, *Habeas Corpus Checklist* (West Group 1998).

159. 510 U.S. 266 (1994).

160. *Id.* at 270 n.4. Some courts had also required the challenged governmental conduct to be "egregious." *Id.*

161. Martin A. Schwartz & John E. Kirklin, 1A Section 1983 Litigation: Claims & Defenses, § 3.20, at 315 n.699 (3d ed. 1997).

that the prisoner did not have a cognizable malicious prosecution claim under 42 U.S.C. § 1983 because he failed to establish that prior criminal proceedings had been terminated in his favor.

Both cases merit scrutiny because *Heck* surprisingly looked to the common law to determine whether there was an actionable claim and because *Albright* produced *six* different views as to how to examine the facts of an alleged malicious prosecution claim.

Prior to *Heck*, the Court had derived standards for examining constitutional claims under § 1983 from constitutional amendments, not from common law.[162] It had also held that prisoners could challenge their confinement only under 29 U.S.C. § 2254, not 42 U.S.C. § 1983.[163] In *Heck*, the Court limited potential § 1983 actions by holding that only when a damage action does not undermine the state's authority to confine prisoners may the malicious prosecution action lie under § 1983. [164] The Court used § 2254 as an analogy, noting that no intrusion on a state's authority occurs when "the conviction or sentence has been reversed on direct appeal, expunged by executive order, declared invalid by a state tribunal authorized to make such determination, or called into question by a federal court's issuance of a writ of habeas corpus. . . ."[165]

Similarly, in *Albright*, the Court held that a claim of malicious prosecution is not actionable under the substantive due process component of the Fourteenth Amendment, but suggested that it may be actionable under the Fourth Amendment.[166] Albright, who was the subject of an arrest warrant for selling drugs, surrendered custody and complied with a limit on his traveling outside the state. At a preliminary hearing, a judge determined that the alleged selling of a powder that looked like cocaine was not a state crime.

The Court held that Albright's malicious prosecution claim was not actionable under the substantive due process component of the Fourteenth Amendment. Interestingly, the discussion of substantive due proc-

---

162. *See, e.g.*, Daniels v. Williams, 474 U.S. 327, 331 (1986).

163. Preiser v. Rodriguez, 411 U.S. 475, 488–90 (1973).

164. *Heck*, 114 S. Ct. at 2373.

165. *Id.* at 2372. *See generally* Edwards v. Balisok, 117 S. Ct. 1584, 1589 (1997) (holding that prisoner's alleged procedural due process violation, for which he sought declaratory relief and money damages, is not cognizable under § 1983 because it "necessarily [implies] the invalidity of the punishment imposed").

166. 510 U.S. 266, 275 (1994) (plurality opinion).

ess resulted in the justices expressing six very different views of the facts and the law of substantive due process. The plurality opinion by Chief Justice William H. Rehnquist (joined by Justices O'Connor, Scalia, and Ginsburg) rejected substantive due process as a base for this claim and interpreted the record as not alleging a violation of procedural due process or of a Fourth Amendment right. Justice Rehnquist noted that the lower courts had differing views as to what a plaintiff must allege to state a constitutional claim for "malicious prosecution."[167] Some courts had held that the constitutional claim was identical to the common-law claim; others had required the plaintiff to establish some type of egregious conduct.[168] Justice Rehnquist also stated that the Fourth Amendment applied to "pretrial deprivations of liberty,"[169] but expressed no view as to whether the plaintiff's allegations stated a claim under the Fourth Amendment.

Justice Antonin Scalia, concurring, also rejected substantive due process as a basis for this suit. He reiterated his strong opposition to the Court using substantive due process when a plaintiff alleges "unspecified" liberty interests.[170]

Justice Ruth Bader Ginsburg, in her concurring opinion, interpreted the Fourth Amendment to apply to the facts of this case. She found that the restraint imposed upon Albright constituted a Fourth Amendment seizure, and suggested that the basis of his claim may have been that the arresting officer was responsible for "effectuating and maintaining" the seizure.[171]

Justice Anthony M. Kennedy, joined by Justice Clarence Thomas, concurred in the judgment, holding that a malicious prosecution claim is one actually alleging a violation of procedural due process.[172] In contrast to Justice Scalia, however, Justice Kennedy affirmed that the due process clause protects more than the liberty interests specified in the Bill of Rights. He stated that "the due process requirements for criminal proceedings do not include a standard for the initiation of a criminal prose-

---

167. *Id.* at 270 n.4.
168. *Id.*
169. *Id.* at 274.
170. *Id.* at 275 (Scalia, J., concurring).
171. *Id.* at 279 n.5 (Ginsburg, J., concurring).
172. *Id.* at 285 (Kennedy, J., concurring).

cution."[173] Justice Kennedy stated that, in some circumstances, the challenged governmental actions may state a violation of procedural due process, but found that such a claim was not viable in this case because state law provided the plaintiff with a remedy.

Justice David H. Souter rejected the substantive due process claim for two reasons. First, such a claim is available only when another amendment does not apply and the claim is "substantial."[174] Justice Souter thought that judicial "self-restraint" is necessary when examining this type of claim. Second, the types of injuries alleged were compensable under the Fourth Amendment. The plaintiff had alleged the following damages:

> . . . limitations of his liberty, freedom of association, and freedom of movement by virtue of the terms of his bond; financial expense of his legal defense; reputational harm among members of the community; inability to transact business or obtain employment in his local area, necessitating relocation to St. Louis; inability to secure credit; and personal pain and suffering.[175]

Justice Souter recognized that sometimes injuries may occur before there is a Fourth Amendment seizure; whether these injuries are actionable under substantive due process, he stated, was not addressed by the facts of this case.

In contrast to the other justices, Justice John Paul Stevens, joined by Justice Harry A. Blackmun, concluded that the plaintiff had stated a violation of substantive due process.[176] He found the officer's conduct shocking, and he stated that the Bill of Rights specifically protects against pretrial deprivations of liberty. Using the grand jury clause of the Fifth Amendment, Justice Stevens reasoned that the liberty interest is specified by the Constitution. Even though states are not required to use grand juries, the presence of this clause helped to define the word "liberty" for Justice Stevens. He also noted that in criminal procedure cases the Court "has identified numerous violations of due process that have no counterparts in the specific guarantees of the Bill of Rights."[177]

---

173. *Id.* at 283.
174. *Id.* at 288 (Souter, J., concurring).
175. *Id.* at 289 (Souter, J., concurring).
176. *Id.* at 302 (Stevens, J., dissenting).
177. *Id.* at 304.

Thus, although a majority of the Court held that malicious prosecution claims were not viable substantive due process claims, there was no clear majority with respect to the constitutional basis for these claims. If, however, Justice Souter's opinion can be interpreted as establishing such claims under the Fourth Amendment, then a majority of the Court would likely find these claims actionable under the Fourth Amendment.

In response to *Albright*, some courts have held that abuse of criminal process can raise a procedural due process claim [178] or a Fourth Amendment claim requiring the plaintiff to prove "the perversion of proper legal procedures."[179]

Conditions-of-Confinement Claims Under the Eighth Amendment

When challenging their conditions of confinement, prisoners must prove that the conditions constituted "cruel and unusual punishment" within the meaning of the Eighth Amendment. The Supreme Court has defined this standard as containing both subjective and objective components. [180] The subjective component requires proof that officials acted with subjective deliberative indifference;[181] the objective component requires proof that the deprivation was sufficiently serious.[182] Several Supreme Court decisions shed light on the meaning of these two elements.

In *Estelle v. Gamble*,[183] a case involving medical care of prisoners, the Supreme Court held that, to state a claim under the Eighth Amendment, a prisoner must prove that officials were deliberately indifferent to the

---

178. *See, e.g.,* Cook v. Sheldon, 41 F.3d 73 (2d Cir. 1994).

179. Singer v. Fulton County Sheriff, 63 F.3d 110, 117 (2d Cir. 1995). Professor Martin A. Schwartz has argued that the Second Circuit's five factors for Fourth Amendment malicious prosecution claims are more stringent than the common-law tort: "(1) A deprivation of liberty; (2) Resulting from a governmental seizure; (3) In the form of legal process; (4) Without probable cause or otherwise unreasonable; and (5) Termination of the criminal proceeding in favor of the accused." Martin A. Schwartz & John E. Kirklin, 1A Section 1983 Litigation: Claims and Defenses, § 3.20, at 325 (3d ed. 1997) (citing *Singer*, 63 F.3d at 118). Schwartz and Kirklin add that this type of claim is not a challenge to the decision to prosecute, but rather to the seizure arising "from legal process." *Id.*

180. *See, e.g.,* Farmer v. Brennan, 114 S. Ct. 1970, 1977 (1994); Wilson v. Seiter, 501 U.S. 294, 302–03 (1991).

181. *Farmer*, 114 S. Ct. at 1977.

182. *Wilson*, 501 U.S. at 302–03.

183. 429 U.S. 97, 106 (1976).

prisoner's "serious" medical needs.[184] It determined that the Eighth Amendment was not violated by negligent medical care.

Fifteen years later, in *Wilson v. Seiter*,[185] a divided Court interpreted *Estelle* to govern all claims challenging prison conditions. A majority of the Court narrowly defined both the subjective and objective components. The Court held that the subjective component is a necessary element of all prison conditions claims. Inhumane prison conditions alone do not constitute an Eighth Amendment violation. The Court also held that the objective component requires proof that the deprivation was "serious," that is, one addressing a basic human need, such as "food, warmth, or exercise."[186] "Nothing so amorphous as 'overall conditions' can rise to the level of cruel and unusual punishment when no specific deprivation of a single human needs exists."[187] With these requirements, the Court left open whether inadequate funding was a defense to a finding of subjective deliberate indifference.[188] The dissent, however, noted that the courts of appeals have rejected such a "cost" defense.[189]

Subsequently, the Supreme Court held in *Helling v. McKinney*[190] that a prisoner had stated an Eighth Amendment claim in challenging his confinement with a prisoner who smoked five packages of cigarettes a day. [191] The Court held that this case was similar to *Estelle* because the challenge concerned the prisoner's health. The Court explained that the Eighth Amendment is not limited only to claims involving current physical harm: The Eighth Amendment also applies to conditions that may cause harm to prisoners in the future.

In *Farmer v. Brennan*,[192] the Supreme Court defined the term "deliberate indifference."[193] Recognizing a duty on the part of prison officials to protect prisoners from harming each other, the Court explained that the "deliberate indifference" standard in this context is subjective, not objective. Subjective deliberate indifference requires proof that the official ac-

---

184. *Id.*
185. 501 U.S. 294, 302–04 (1991).
186. *Id.* at 304–05.
187. *Id.* at 305.
188. *Id.*
189. *Id.* at 311 n.2 (White, J., dissenting).
190. 113 S. Ct. 2475 (1993).
191. *Id.* at 2480–82.
192. 114 S. Ct. 1970 (1994).
193. *Id.* at 1984.

tually knew of a substantial risk of serious harm and failed to act.[194] Objective deliberate indifference, on the other hand, does not require proof of the actor's state of mind; it is established by showing that officials knew or should have known of the harm.[195] To explain its standard, the Court offered two comments. First, subjective deliberate indifference protects the prison official who failed to deduce the risk of serious harm because the official, in fact, did not know of the harm.[196] Second, the jury can make an inference that the official actually knew of the risk,[197] based on the same type of circumstantial evidence that is used to prove objective deliberate indifference.

The subjective and objective components of the analysis of conditions-of-confinement claims under the Eighth Amendment are also a part of the Court's analysis of excessive force claims under the Eighth Amendment. In *Hudson v. McMillian*,[198] the Court held that the subjective component required proof that the prison officials acted maliciously. The Court added that proof of malicious conduct automatically establishes the objective component, as long as there was more than a de minimus injury.[199]

The Court has thus recognized two different subjective components under the Eighth Amendment—deliberate indifference and malice.[200] Malice is the proper standard in the prison discipline or riot contexts because exigencies exist; however, in general prison conditions litigation, where prison officials do not encounter these difficult circumstances, deliberate indifference is the proper standard.[201] The Court derived these different states of mind by balancing a prisoner's interest in bodily integrity against the need for institutional order.

First Amendment Claims

Two frequently raised claims by government employees involve the First Amendment, which safeguards the right to free speech. The first claim

---

194. *Id.*
195. *Id.* at 1978.
196. *Id.*
197. *Id.* at 1982 n.8
198. 112 S. Ct. 995, 999 (1992).
199. *Id.* at 1000. *See also supra* text accompanying note 151.
200. *Id.* at 998–99.
201. *Id.*

addresses adverse employment decisions that were based on employees' affiliations with political parties. The second claim questions decisions based upon employees' speech. To resolve these claims, the Supreme Court has provided general guidelines for balancing the interests of the parties.

Political Patronage Claims

In four decisions, the Supreme Court has limited the circumstances under which public employers may make political patronage the dispositive reason for adverse employment decisions. A plurality of the Court first held, in *Elrod v. Burns*,[202] that patronage dismissals must be limited to "policy-making positions." Four years later, in *Branti v. Finkel*,[203] the Supreme Court rejected the *Elrod* rule, stating that "the ultimate inquiry is not whether the label 'policymaker' or 'confidential' fits a particular position," but whether the hiring authority can demonstrate that party affiliation is "an appropriate requirement for the effective performance of the public office involved."[204] The Court also stressed the need to evaluate actual performance in *Rutan v. Republican Party of Illinois*.[205] It held that the First Amendment prohibits political patronage as the sole basis for decisions concerning "promotions, transfers, and recalls after layoffs." The Court explained that deficient performance effectively protects the government's interests when addressing the employment of staff members. When evaluating high-level employees, the government, however, may consider "who will loyally implement its policies."[206]

Although the Court recognized two classes of employees, staff members and high-level employees, it nevertheless explained that performance is the central issue, with patronage being a factor with respect only to the latter group.

The Court recently explained that public contractors may receive the protection afforded staff members in *O'Hare Truck Service Inc. v. Northlake*.[207] The *O'Hare* Court rejected drawing a distinction between inde-

---

202. 427 U.S. 347, 367–68 (1976).
203. 445 U.S. 507 (1980).
204. *Id.* at 518.
205. 497 U.S. 62, 74–75 (1990).
206. *Id.* at 74.
207. 116 S. Ct. 2353, 2358 (1996).

pendent contractors and employees because contractors are not less dependent on government income than are employees.[208]

Free Speech Claims

When public employees claim that their employers made adverse employment decisions because of their speech, two general issues are central: (1) whether their speech was a "matter of public concern" and (2) if so, whether it undermined an effective work environment.[209] The Supreme Court has recognized that both inquiries describe standards, not rules, that must be applied to the facts of each case.

The First Amendment requires balancing the need for employees to speak out on a matter of public concern against the need for an effective working relationship.[210] In determining what constitutes a matter of public concern, courts should consider "the content, form and context" of the statement.[211] Employers need not determine what the employee actually said;[212] they must only reasonably investigate the nature of the employee's speech.[213] If there was a substantial likelihood that the employee engaged in protected speech, a manager must investigate before making an adverse employment decision regarding the employee.[214] Only procedures outside the range of what a reasonable manager would use indicate a violation. The reasonableness standard is objective; the subjective good faith of the employer is not controlling.[215]

There are two situations, however, where speech on a matter of public concern may nevertheless be unprotected under the First Amendment: employment relationships that require confidentiality, and those that require harmony because of the "personal or intimate" nature of the work.[216] In evaluating the second prong—disruptiveness—courts are to show "wide deference to the employer's judgment" when "a close work-

---

208. *Id.* at 2359–60.
209. Pickering v. Board of Educ., 391 U.S. 563, 568 (1968).
210. *Id.* at 568.
211. Connick v. Meyers, 461 U.S. 138, 147–48 (1983).
212. Waters v. Churchill, 114 S. Ct. 1878, 1889–90 (1994) (O'Connor, J.) (plurality opinion joined by Chief Justice Rehnquist and Justices Souter and Ginsburg).
213. *Id.*
214. *Id.* at 1889 (plurality opinion).
215. *Id.*
216. Pickering v. Board of Educ., 391 U.S. 563, 570 n.3 (1968).

ing relationship [is] essential to fulfilling public responsibilities."[217] If, however, an employee does not have a "confidential, policymaking, or public contact role," the level of disruptiveness would probably be "minimal."[218]

Dismissal based on pretextual reasons, however, is impermissible.[219] For example, if an employer fires an employee not because of unprotected, disruptive statements, but because of protected, nondisruptive speech, then the employer has violated the employee's First Amendment rights.

When considering both free speech and political patronage claims under the First Amendment, the dominant inquiry includes consideration of the employee's job and the effective performance of the government. With respect to free speech claims, the First Amendment applies only if the speech covered a matter of public concern. The First Amendment, however, does not create a property or liberty right to a job. It simply ensures that the governmental employer does not make adverse employment decisions that violate a person's right to free speech.

Dormant Commerce Clause Claims

Violations of the dormant commerce clause are generally actionable under § 1983. Article I, § 8, cl.3 confers power upon Congress to regulate interstate commerce; it also acts as a restraint on state regulations even when Congress has not regulated in the area. In *Dennis v. Higgins*,[220] the Supreme Court held that the commerce clause is not only a "power-allocating provision, giving Congress preemptive authority," but is also a provision that confers rights, privileges, and immunities within the meaning of 42 U.S.C. § 1983.[221] Courts may award declaratory and injunctive relief for dormant commerce clause violations.[222]

---

217. Connick v. Meyers, 461 U.S. 138, 147–48 (1982).

218. Rankin v. McPherson, 483 U.S. 378, 390–91 (1987).

219. Waters v. Churchill, 114 S. Ct. 1878, 1889 (1994) (citing Mount Healthy City Sch. Dist. Bd. of Educ. v. Doyle, 429 U.S. 274 (1977)) (First Amendment free speech claim required determining whether the plaintiff was fired because of protected or unprotected speech).

220. 498 U.S. 439 (1991).

221. *Id.* at 447.

222. *Id.* at 451.

The *Higgins* Court held that there was an implied right under the commerce clause. To determine whether this right was implied, the Court applied the three-part test it has used in determining whether rights under federal statutes are actionable under § 1983: (1) whether the provision "creates obligations binding on the governmental unit"; (2) whether the plaintiff's interest is "too vague and amorpho us"; and (3) whether the provision was designed to benefit the plaintiff.[223] The Court found the dormant commerce clause was intended to create individual rights, even though Congress may at any time eliminate the right by using its plenary powers.

Dormant commerce clause claims, however, are generally not actionable in federal or state court when the claims involve challenges to the state tax scheme. In *National Private Truck Council, Inc. v. Oklahoma Tax Commission*,[224] the Court articulated an exception to *Higgins*: § 1983 does not authorize federal or state courts to issue declaratory and injunctive relief in dormant commerce clause cases when state law provides an "adequate remedy at law."[225] In federal court, such relief is inappropr iate because of the principles of comity and federalism, and the Tax Injunction Act.[226] In state court, declaratory and injunctive relief are inappropriate under § 1983 because Congress did not intend for state courts to intrude into state taxing schemes when an adequate legal remedy exists.

---

223. *Id.* at 448–49 (quoting Golden State Transit Corp. v. Los Angeles, 493 U.S. 103, 106 (1989)).

224. 515 U.S. 582 (1995).

225. *Id.* at 588.

226. *Id.* at 586.

Chapter 4

Deprivation of Federal Statutory Rights

Maine v. Thiboutot: *"Plain Language" Approach*

The "and laws" phrase in § 1983 affords a remedy for the deprivation of some federal statutory rights, as well as federal constitutional rights. In *Maine v. Thiboutot,*[227] the State of Maine and its commissioner of human services had allegedly deprived certain individuals of welfare benefits to which they were entitled under the Social Security Act.[228] The Supreme Court, emphasizing that Congress had not attached any modifiers to the phrase "and laws," held, over a strong dissent,[229] that the phrase "means what it says" and that "the plain language of [§ 1983] undoubtedly embraces [the] claim that [state officials] violated the Social Security Act."[230]

Defining the Limits of "And Laws" Actions

Since *Thiboutot,* the Supreme Court has decided a number of cases in which it has attempted to define the limits of "and laws" actions under

---

227. 448 U.S. 1 (1980).

228. *See* 42 U.S.C. §§ 301–1397f (1988 & Supp. V).

229. Justice Lewis F. Powell, Jr., with whom Chief Justice Warren E. Burger and then-Justice William Rehnquist joined, concluded that the historical evidence convincingly showed that the phrase "and laws," as used in § 1983, "was—and remains—nothing more than a shorthand reference to equal rights legislation enacted by Congress." *Thiboutot,* 448 U.S. at 12 (Powell, J., dissenting).

230. *Thiboutot,* 448 U.S. at 4.

§ 1983. The Court recently summarized the principles it has developed for "and laws" actions as follows:

> In order to seek redress through § 1983 . . . a plaintiff must assert the violation of a federal *right*, not merely a violation of federal *law*. We have traditionally looked at three factors when determining whether a particular statutory provision gives rise to a federal right. First, Congress must have intended that the provision in question benefit the plaintiff. Second, the plaintiff must demonstrate that the right assertedly protected by the statute is not so "vague and amorphous" that its enforcement would strain judicial competence. Third, the statute must unambiguously impose a binding obligation on the States. In other words, the provision giving rise to the asserted right must be couched in mandatory rather than precatory terms.
>
> Even if a plaintiff demonstrates that a federal statute creates an individual right, there is only a rebuttable presumption that the right is enforceable under § 1983. Because our inquiry focuses on congressional intent, dismissal is proper if Congress "specifically foreclosed a remedy under § 1983." Congress may do so expressly, by forbidding recourse to § 1983 in the statute itself, or impliedly, by creating a comprehensive enforcement scheme that is incompatible with individual enforcement under § 1983.[231]

Thus the two major issues for § 1983 "and laws" cases are whether a federal statute creates an enforceable right and whether Congress foreclosed the § 1983 lawsuit by enacting a comprehensive scheme in the federal statute.

Enforceable Rights

The most difficult question for "and laws" cases is whether the relevant federal statute creates an enforceable right actionable under § 1983. At issue in *Pennhurst State School & Hospital v. Halderman*[232] was whether 42 U.S.C. § 6009, the "bill of rights" provision of the Developmental Disabilities Assistance and Bill of Rights Act, created enforceable rights in favor of the developmentally disabled.[233] The Court identified the correct inquiry as whether the provision "imposed an obligation on the States to

---

231. Blessing v. Freestone, 117 S. Ct. 1353, 1359–60 (1997) (emphasis in original; cites omitted).

232. 451 U.S. 1 (1981).

233. *Id.* at 15 (citing former § 6010, which is now § 6009).

spend state money to fund certain rights as a condition of receiving federal moneys under the Act or whether it spoke merely in precatory terms."[234] Noting that "if Congress intends to impose a condition on the grant of federal moneys, it must do so unambiguously[,]"[235] the Court concluded that "the provisions of § [6009] were intended to be hortatory, not mandatory."[236] "Congress intended to encourage, rather than mandate, the provision of better services to the developmentally disabled."[237] Accordingly, § 6009 did not create substantive rights in favor of the mentally disabled to "appropriate treatment" in the "least restrictive" environment, and thus was not enforceable through § 1983.[238]

In the next several decisions, the Supreme Court found that federal statutes created enforceable rights. For example, in *Golden State Transit Corp. v. Los Angeles,*[239] the Court held that Golden State could sue for damages under § 1983 to remedy the violation of its right under the National Labor Relations Act[240] not to have the renewal of its taxi license conditioned on the settlement of a pending labor dispute.[241]

Similarly, in *Wright v. City of Roanoke Redevelopment & Housing Authority,*[242] the Court determined that regulations created enforceable rights. The defendant was a public housing authority subject to the Brooke Amendment's "ceiling for rents charged to low-income people living in public housing projects."[243] The Department of Housing and Urban Development ("HUD") had, in its implementing regulations, "consistently considered 'rent' to include a reasonable amount for the use of utilities,"[244] which reasonable amount did "not include charges for utility consumption in excess of the public housing agency's schedule of allowances for utility consumption."[245] Renters brought suit under § 1983 alleging that the Housing Authority had "imposed a surcharge for

---

234. *Id.* at 18.
235. *Id.* at 17.
236. *Id.* at 24.
237. *Id.* at 20.
238. *Id.* at 10–11.
239. 493 U.S. 103 (1989).
240. *See* 29 U.S.C. §§ 151–169 (1988 & Supp. V).
241. *Golden State*, 493 U.S. at 112–13.
242. 479 U.S. 418 (1987).
243. *Id.* at 420 (citations omitted).
244. *Id.*
245. *Id.* at 421 n.3.

'excess' utility consumption that should have been part of petitioners' rent and deprived them of their statutory right to pay only the prescribed maximum portion of their income as rent." [246] The Court determined that the HUD regulations gave low-income tenants specific and definable rights to a reasonable utility allowance that were enforceable under § 1983, and that the regulations were fully authorized by the statute. [247]

The Court in *Wilder v. Virginia Hospital Ass'n*[248] also found an enforceable right as it examined the Boren Amendment to the Medicaid Act,[249] which requires a participating state to reimburse health care providers at "reasonable rates."[250] The Court concluded that health care providers were clearly intended beneficiaries of the Boren Amendment, [251] that the amendment was cast in mandatory terms, imposing a "binding obligation" on participating states to adopt reasonable rates of reimbursement for health care providers, and that this obligation was enforceable under § 1983.[252] Rejecting the argument that the obligation imposed by the Boren Amendment was "too vague and amorphous" to be "capable of judicial enforcement,"[253] the Court noted that "the statute and regulations set out factors which a State must consider in adopting its rates," including "the objective benchmark of an 'efficiently and economically operated facility' providing care in compliance with federal and state standards while at the same time ensuring 'reasonable access' to eligible participants."[254]

In contrast, the Court in *Suter v. Artist M.*[255] did not find an enforceable right as it considered a provision of the Adoption Assistance and Child Welfare Act of 1980.[256] The Act provides for federal reimbursement of certain expenses incurred by a state in administering foster care and adoption services, conditioned upon the state's submission of a plan

---

246. *Id.* at 421.
247. *Id.* at 430.
248. 496 U.S. 498 (1990).
249. *See* 42 U.S.C. §§ 1396–1396v (1998 & Supp. V).
250. 42 U.S.C. § 1396a(a)(13)(A) (1998 & Supp. V).
251. *Wilder*, 496 U.S. at 510.
252. *Id.* at 512.
253. *Id.* at 519.
254. *Id.*
255. 503 U.S. 347 (1992).
256. *Id.* at 350. *See* 42 U.S.C. §§ 620–628, 670–679a (1988 & Supp. V).

for approval by the Secretary of Health and Human Services.[257] To be approved, the plan must satisfy certain requirements, including one that mandates that the state make "reasonable efforts" to keep children in their homes.[258]

The issue before the Court was whether "Congress, in enacting the Adoption Act, unambiguously conferr[ed] upon the child beneficiaries of the Act a right to enforce the requirement that the State make 'reasonable efforts' to prevent a child from being removed from his home, and once removed to reunify the child with his family."[259] The Court held that it did not. The Court concluded that the only unambiguous requirement imposed by 42 U.S.C. § 671(a) was that the state submit a plan to be approved by the secretary.[260]

The Court emphasized that in *Wilder* it had "relied in part on the fact that the statute and regulations set forth in some detail the factors to be considered in determining the methods for calculating rates,"[261] whereas in the instant case the Child Welfare Act contained "[n]o further statutory guidance . . . as to how 'reasonable efforts' are to be measured."[262]

---

257. 42 U.S.C. §§ 620–628, 670–679a (1988 & Supp. V).

258. 42 U.S.C. § 671(a)(15) (1988).

259. *Suter*, 503 U.S. at 357.

260. *Id.*

261. *Id.* at 359.

262. *Id.* at 360. Congress responded to *Suter* by passing an amendment to the Social Security Act which provides that in all pending and future actions

> brought to enforce a provision of the Social Security Act, such provision is not to be deemed unenforceable because of its inclusion in a section of the Act requiring a State plan or specifying the required contents of a State plan. This section is not intended to limit or expand the grounds for determining the availability of private actions to enforce State plan requirements other than by overturn ing any such grounds applied in Suter v. Artist M. [cite omitted], but not applied in prior Supreme Court decisions respecting such enforceability; provided, however, that this section is not intended to alter the holding in Suter v. Artist M. that section 471(a)(15) [42 U.S.C. § 671(a)(15)] of the Act is not enforceable in a private right of action.

42 U.S.C. § 1320a-2 (amended October 20, 1994).

Thus, while the holding of *Suter* with respect to the "reasonable efforts" provision remains good law, "the amendment overrules the general theory in *Suter* that the only private right of action available under a statute requiring a state plan is an action against the state for not having that plan. Instead, the previous tests of *Wilder* and *Pennhurst* apply to the question of whether or not the particulars of a state plan can be enforced by its intended beneficiaries." Jeanine B. v. Thompson, 877 F. Supp. 1268, 1283 (E.D. Wis. 1995).

Wilder *and* Suter *Synthesized*

Courts of appeals have uniformly taken the position that the holdings of *Wilder* and *Suter* can and should be synthesized.[263] Later, in *Livadas v. Bradshaw*,[264] the Supreme Court held that the plaintiff had an enforceable right under the National Labor Relations Act "to complete the collective bargaining process and agree to an arbitration clause."[265] The Court observed that "apart from . . . exceptional cases, § 1983 remains a generally and presumptively available remedy for claimed violations of federal law."[266]

In *Blessing v. Freestone*,[267] a unanimous Court rejected an attempt by custodial parents to enforce, through a § 1983 action, a general, undifferentiated right to "substantial compliance" by state officials with a federally funded child-support enforcement program that operates under Title IV-D of the Social Security Act.[268] While the Court did not foreclose the possibility that certain provisions of Title IV-D might give rise to private, enforceable rights, it faulted the court of appeals for taking a "blanket approach" and for painting "with too broad a brush" in determining whether Title IV-D creates enforceable rights.[269] The case was remanded, and plaintiffs were advised to articulate with particularity the rights they were seeking to enforce. *Blessing* will force plaintiffs to break their claims down into "manageable analytic bites" so that the court can "ascertain

---

263. *See, e.g.*, Wood v. Tompkins, 33 F.3d 600, 606 (6th Cir. 1994) ("*Suter* majority expressly relied on parts of *Wilder*, carefully distinguished other parts, did not overrule the earlier case, and is entirely consistent with it."); Lampkin v. District of Columbia, 27 F.3d 605, 610 (D.C. Cir. 1994) (synthesizing *Suter* and *Wilder*); Miller v. Whitburn, 10 F.3d 1315, 1319 (7th Cir. 1993) (*Suter* "is not the death knell of the analytic framework established in *Wilder*"); Marshall v. Switzer, 10 F.3d 925, 928 (2d Cir. 1993) (synthesizing *Suter* and *Wilder*); Arkansas Med. Soc'y, Inc. v. Reynolds, 6 F.3d 519, 525 (8th Cir. 1993) ("We choose to synthesize the two cases by proceeding with the two-step *Golden State* analysis used in *Wilder*, bearing in mind the additional considerations mandated by *Suter*."); Stowell v. Ives, 976 F.2d 65, 68 (1st Cir. 1992) (finding it "both prudent and possible to synthesize the teachings of *Suter* with the Court's prior precedents").

264. 114 S. Ct. 2068 (1994).

265. *Id.* at 2083–84.

266. *Id.*

267. 117 S. Ct. 1353 (1997).

268. Title IV-D of the Social Security Act, as added, 88 Stat. 2351 and as amended, 42 U.S.C.A. §§ 651–669b (Supp. 1997).

269. *Blessing*, 117 S. Ct. at 1360–61.

48

whether each separate claim satisfies the various criteria [the Supreme Court has] set forth for determining whether a federal statute creates rights."[270]

Comprehensive Scheme: Congress's Intent to Foreclose

The Supreme Court recently explained that unless the federal statute under consideration "expressly curtails § 1983 actions,"[271] officials trying to establish Congress's intent to foreclose must "make the difficult showing that allowing § 1983 actions to go forward in these circumstances 'would be inconsistent with Congress's carefully tailored scheme.'"[272] In only two cases—*Middlesex County Sewerage Authority v. National Sea Clammers Ass'n*[273] and *Smith v. Robinson*[274]—has the Court determined that comprehensive schemes within a statute foreclosed the § 1983 lawsuit.

In *Sea Clammers,* an association claimed that the County Sewerage Authority discharged and dumped pollutants, violating the Federal Water Pollution Control Act[275] and the Marine Protection, Research, and Sanctuaries Act of 1972.[276] In addition, the County Sewerage Authority allegedly violated the terms of their permits.[277] Although the issue before the Court was "whether [the Association] may raise either of these claims in a private suit for injunctive and monetary relief, where such a suit is not expressly authorized by either of these Acts,"[278] the Court addressed, *sua sponte*, the enforceability of these Acts pursuant to § 1983. Noting that both statutes contained "unusually elaborate enforcement provisions[,]"[279] the Court held that "[w]hen the remedial devices provided in a particular Act are sufficiently comprehensive, they may suffice to dem-

---

270. *Id.* at 1360.

271. *Id.* at 1362.

272. *Id.* (quoting Golden State Transit Corp. v. Los Angeles, 493 U.S. 103, 107 (1989)).

273. 453 U.S. 1 (1981).

274. 468 U.S. 992 (1984).

275. *See* 33 U.S.C. §§ 1251–1387 (1988 & Supp. V).

276. *See* 33 U.S.C. §§ 1401–1445 (1988 & Supp. V).

277. *Sea Clammers*, 453 U.S. at 12.

278. *Id.*

279. *Id.* at 13.

onstrate congressional intent to preclude the remedy of suits under § 1983."[280]

Similarly, in *Smith* the Court concluded that the "carefully tailored administrative and judicial mechanism"[281] embodied in the Education of the Handicapped Act (EHA)[282] reflected Congressional intent that the EHA be "the exclusive avenue through which a plaintiff may assert an equal protection claim to a publicly financed special education."[283] The dissent disagreed:

> The natural resolution of the conflict between the EHA [renamed IDEA], on the one hand, and . . . [section] 1983, on the other, is to require a plaintiff with a claim covered by the EHA to pursue relief through the administrative channels established by that Act before seeking redress in the courts under . . . [section] 1983.[284]

The dissent's position became the law when, in response to *Smith*, Congress amended the EHA to provide explicitly that parallel constitutional claims were not preempted by the EHA and could be raised in conjunction with claims based upon it.[285]

Except for these two cases, the Court has determined that the federal statutes under consideration did not foreclose a § 1983 lawsuit.[286]

---

280. *Id.* at 20.

281. *Smith*, 468 U.S. at 992.

282. *See* 20 U.S.C. §§ 1400–1485 (1988 & Supp. V). In 1991 the Act was renamed Individuals With Disabilities Education Act (IDEA), 20 U.S.C. §§ 1400–1491 (1994).

283. *Smith*, 468 U.S. at 1009.

284. *Id.* at 1024 (Brennan, J., joined by Marshall, J. and Stevens, J., dissenting).

285. *See* 20 U.S.C. § 1415(f) (1988 & Supp. V).

286. *See, e.g.,* Blessing v. Freestone, 117 S. Ct. 1353, 1362 (1997); Wilder v. Virginia Hosp. Ass'n, 496 U.S. 498, 522–23 (1990); Wright v. City of Roanoke Redev. & Hous. Auth., 479 U.S. 418, 425 (1987).

Chapter 5

Governmental and Supervisory Liability

State Liability: Eleventh Amendment Immunity and Status as "Person" Under § 1983

The Eleventh Amendment[287] shields a state from suit in federal court unless the state consents to suit[288] or waives its immunity.[289] A damages action against a state official, in his or her official capacity, is tantamount to a suit against the state itself and, absent waiver or consent, would be barred by the Eleventh Amendment as well.[290] Although Congress may

---

287. "The Judicial Power of the United States shall not be construed to extend to any suit in law or equity, commenced or prosecuted against one of the United States by Citizens of another State, or by Citizens or Subjects of any Foreign State." U.S. Const. amend. XI.

In *Hans v. Louisiana*, 134 U.S. 1 (1890), the amendment was interpreted to prohibit suits in federal court against a state by citizens of the defendant state.

288. A state's consent to suit must be unequivocally expressed. Edelman v. Jordan, 415 U.S. 651, 673 (1974).

289. A state's waiver of sovereign immunity in its own state courts is not a waiver of Eleventh Amendment immunity in the federal courts. Florida Dep't of Health v. Florida Nursing Home Ass'n, 450 U.S. 147, 150 (1981) (per curiam).

290. In *Ex Parte Young*, 209 U.S. 123 (1908), the Supreme Court held that a state official who acted unconstitutionally could be sued in his official capacity for prospective relief. Such a suit "does not affect the State in its sovereign or governmental capacity" because the official who commits an unconstitutional act is deemed "stripped of his official or representative character . . . ." *Id.* at 159–60.

The Eleventh Amendment bars prospective relief sought against state officials in their official capacity where supplemental jurisdiction is asserted to enforce conformity with

expressly abrogate a state's Eleventh Amendment immunity pursuant to its enforcement power under section 5 of the Fourteenth Amendment,[291] Congress did not do so in passing § 1983.[292] Thus the Eleventh Amendment is applicable to § 1983 litigation. Even if a third party indemnifies a state, the Eleventh Amendment still applies and protects the state from an adverse judgment.[293]

A question often raised is whether certain subdivisions, boards, or agencies are considered "arm[s] of the State" for Eleventh Amendment purposes. In *Mount Healthy City School District Board of Education v. Doyle*,[294] the Supreme Court looked, in part, to the nature of the entity created by state law and held that a local school district was not an "arm of the State" where Ohio law characterized the local school district as a political subdivision.[295] In *Lake Country Estates, Inc. v. Tahoe Regional Planning Agency*,[296] the Supreme Court followed the *Mount Healthy* approach and adopted a presumption that an interstate compact agency would not be entitled to Eleventh Amendment immunity "[u]nless there is good reason to believe that the States structured the new agency to enable it to enjoy the special constitutional protection of the States themselves, and that Congress concurred in that purpose . . . ."[297]

provisions of *state* law. Pennhurst State Sch. & Hosp. v. Halderman, 465 U.S. 89, 106 (1984). Where a state has waived its Eleventh Amendment immunity, however, and consented to suit, a state may be named as a defendant on a state law claim (e.g., *respondeat superior*), where that claim is part of the same "case or controversy" as the § 1983 claim(s) against the state actors sued in their individual capacities. Rosen v. Chang, 758 F. Supp. 799, 803–04 (D.R.I. 1991).

291. Fitzpatrick v. Bitzer, 427 U.S. 445 (1976). *Cf. Seminole Tribe v. Florida*, 116 S. Ct. 1114 (1996), holding that Congress had no power under the Commerce Clause to abrogate states' Eleventh Amendment immunity.

292. Quern v. Jordan, 440 U.S. 332, 342 (1979).

293. Regents of the University of California v. Doe, 117 S. Ct. 900, 905 (1997).

294. 429 U.S. 274 (1977).

295. *Id.* at 280. *Compare* Martinez v. Board of Educ., 748 F.2d 1393, 1396 (10th Cir. 1984) (school districts in New Mexico are "arms of the State"), *with* Daddow v. Carlsbad Mun. Sch. Dist., 898 F.2d 1235 (D. N.M. 1995) (local board of education in New Mexico is not "arm of the State"), *cert. denied*, 116 S. Ct. 753 (1996).

296. 440 U.S. 391 (1979).

297. *Id.* at 401. See also *Hess v. Port Authority Trans-Hudson Corp.*, 513 U.S. 30 (1994), where the Court held that injured railroad workers could assert a federal statutory right, under the FELA, to recover damages against the Port Authority and that concerns underlying the Eleventh Amendment—"the States' solvency and dignity"—were not touched. *Id.* at 52. The Court noted:

Because the Eleventh Amendment operates to bar suits against states only in federal court, a question emerged as to whether a state could be sued under § 1983 in *state* court. In *Will v. Michigan Department of State Police*,[298] the Court held that neither a state nor a state official in his *official* capacity is a "person" for purposes of a § 1983 damages action.[299] Thus, even if a state is found to have waived its Eleventh Amendment immunity in federal court, or even if a § 1983 action is brought in state court, where the Eleventh Amendment has no applicability, *Will* precludes a damages action against the state governmental entity. This holding does not apply when a state official is sued in his official capacity for prospective injunctive relief.[300]

An official may be a state official for some purposes and a local government official for others. For example, in *McMillian v. Monroe County*,[301] a five-member majority of the Supreme Court held that a county sheriff in Alabama is not a final policymaker for the county in the area of law enforcement.[302] The Court in *McMillian* noted that

> the question is not whether Sheriff Tate acts for Alabama or Monroe County in some categorical, "all or nothing" manner. Our cases on the liability of local governments under § 1983 instruct us to ask whether governmental officials are final policymakers for the local government in a particular area, or on a particular issue. . . . Thus, we are not seeking to make a characterization of Alabama sheriffs that will hold true for every type of official action they engage in. We simply ask whether Sheriff Tate represents the State or the county when he acts in a law enforcement capacity.[303]

The proper focus is not on the use of profits or surplus, but rather is on losses and debts. If the expenditures of the enterprise exceed receipts, is the State in fact obligated to bear and pay the resulting indebtedness of the enterprise? When the answer is "No"—both legally and practically—then the Eleventh Amendment's core concern is not implicated. *Id.* at 51.

See also Harter v. Vernon, 101 F.3d 334, 340 (4th Cir. 1996) ("In sum, when determining if an officer or entity enjoys Eleventh Amendment immunity a court must first establish whether the state treasury will be affected by the lawsuit. If the answer is yes, the officer or entity is immune under the Eleventh Amendment.").

298. 491 U.S. 58 (1989).
299. *Id.* at 71.
300. *Id.* at 71 n.10.
301. 117 S. Ct. 1734 (1997).
302. *Id.* at 1736.
303. *Id.* at 1737.

The Court emphasized the role that state law plays in the court's determination of whether an official has final policy-making authority for a local government entity. As the Court noted, "[t]his is not to say that state law can answer the question for us by, for example, simply labeling as a state official an official who clearly makes county policy. But our understanding of the actual function of a governmental official, in a particular area, will necessarily be dependent on the definition of the official's functions under relevant state law."[304] Thus, Alabama sheriffs, when executing their law-enforcement duties, represent the state of Alabama, not their counties. Even the presence of the following factors was not enough to persuade the majority of the Court otherwise: (1) the sheriff's salary is paid out of the county treasury; (2) the county provides the sheriff with equipment, including cruisers; (3) the sheriff's jurisdiction is limited to the borders of his county; and (4) the sheriff is elected locally by the voters in his county.[305]

In dissent, however, Justice Ginsburg wrote:

> A sheriff locally elected, paid, and equipped, who autonomously sets and implements law enforcement policies operative within the geographic confines of a county, is ordinarily just what he seems to be: a county official. . . . The Court does not appear to question that an Alabama sheriff may still be a county policymaker for some purposes, such as hiring the county's chief jailor. . . . And, as the Court acknowledges, under its approach sheriffs may be policymakers for certain purposes in some States and not in others. . . . The Court's opinion does not call into question the numerous Court of Appeals decisions, some of them decades old, ranking sheriffs as county, not state, policymakers.[306]

In light of *McMillian*, lower courts may need to reconsider their prior determinations as to whether an official represents a state or a county.[307]

---

304. *Id.*

305. *Id.* at 1740.

306. *Id.* at 1746 (Ginsburg, J., joined by Stevens, Souter, & Breyer, JJ., dissenting).

307. *See, e.g.,* Turquitt v. Jefferson County, 137 F. 3d 1285, 1291 (11th Cir. 1998) (en banc) (overruling prior decision that erroneously held that, under Alabama law, a county sheriff was a final policymaker for the county, not for the state, in the area of daily management of jails).

Municipal Liability

No Vicarious Liability

Monell v. Department of Social Services[308] holds that local governments may be liable for damages, as well as declaratory and injunctive relief, whenever "the action that is alleged to be unconstitutional implements or executes a policy statement, ordinance, regulation, or decision officially adopted and promulgated by that body's officers. Moreover . . . local governments . . . may be sued for constitutional deprivations visited pursuant to governmental 'custom' even though such a custom has not received formal approval through the body's official decision-making channels."[309]

Monell rejects government liability based on the doctrine of *respondeat superior*. Thus, a government body cannot be held liable under § 1983 merely because it employs a tortfeasor.[310] *Monell* overruled *Monroe v. Pape*[311] to the extent that *Monroe* had held that local governments could not be sued as "persons" under § 1983.

---

308. 436 U.S. 658 (1978).

309. *Id.* at 690–91. There is conflicting authority as to whether the *Monell* "custom or policy" requirement applies to claims for only prospective relief. In *Los Angeles Police Protective League v. Gates*, 995 F.2d 1469, 1472 (9th Cir. 1993), the majority stated that "the City can be subject to prospective injunctive relief even if the constitutional violation was not the result of an 'official custom or policy'" (citing Chaloux v. Killeen, 886 F.2d 247, 251 (9th Cir. 1989)). In a concurring opinion, however, Judge Fletcher interpreted *Chaloux* as holding that the *Monell* requirement "does not apply to suits against municipalities that seek only prospective relief. . . ." *Gates*, 995 F.2d at 1477. *See also* Nix v. Norman, 879 F.2d 429, 433 (8th Cir. 1989) (insisting that plaintiff in official capacity injunctive relief action satisfy *Monell* official custom or policy requirement).

310. *Monell*, 436 U.S. at 691–92. The Court has held that if there is no constitutional violation, there can be no liability, either on the part of the individual officer or the government body. City of Los Angeles v. Heller, 475 U.S. 796, 799 (1986) ("If a person has suffered no constitutional injury at the hands of the individual police officer, the fact that the departmental regulations might have *authorized* the use of constitutionally excessive force is quite beside the point.") (emphasis in original). *Accord*, Thompson v. Boggs, 33 F.3d 847, 859 (7th Cir. 1994) (where no underlying constitutional violation by officer, no liability on the part of the city or police chief). *But see* Fagan v. City of Vineland, 22 F.3d 1283, 1292 (3d Cir. 1994) ("A finding of municipal liability does not depend automatically or necessarily on the liability of any police officer."). *See also* Mark v. Borough of Hatboro, 51 F.3d 1137, 1153 (3d Cir. 1995) (criticizing the approach of the panel opinion in *Fagan*).

311. 365 U.S. 167 (1961).

Personal and Official Capacity Suits

It is important to understand the difference between personal capacity suits and official capacity suits.[312] When a plaintiff names an official in his individual capacity, the plaintiff is seeking "to impose personal liability upon a government official for actions he takes under color of state law."[313] When a plaintiff names a government official in his official capacity, the plaintiff is seeking to recover compensatory damages from the government body itself.[314] Naming a government official in his official capacity is the equivalent of naming the government entity itself as the defendant, and requires the plaintiff to make out *Monell*-type proof of an official policy or custom as the cause of the constitutional violation. Failure to expressly state that the official is being sued in his individual capacity may be construed as an intent to sue the defendant only in his official capacity.[315] To avoid confusion, where the intended defendant is the government body, the plaintiff should name the entity itself, rather than the individual official in his official capacity.[316]

While qualified immunity is available to an official sued in his personal capacity,[317] there is no qualified immunity available in an official capacity suit. The Supreme Court has held that a local government de-

---

312. *See* Hafer v. Melo, 112 S. Ct. 358, 361–62 (1991) (personal and official capacity suits distinguished).

313. Kentucky v. Graham, 473 U.S. 159, 165 (1985).

314. *See* Brandon v. Holt, 469 U.S. 464, 471–72 (1985); *Kentucky*, 473 U.S. at 159.

315. *See, e.g.,* Wells v. Brown, 891 F.2d 591, 592 (6th Cir. 1989); Nix v. Norman, 879 F.2d 429, 431 (8th Cir. 1989). *But see* Biggs v. Meadows, 66 F.3d 56, 59–60 (4th Cir. 1995) (adopting the view of the majority of circuits, including the Second, Third, Fifth, Seventh, Ninth, Tenth, and Eleventh, that looks to "the substance of the plaintiff's claim, the relief sought, and the course of proceedings to determine the nature of a § 1983 suit when a plaintiff fails to allege capacity. [citing cases] . . . Because we find the majority view to be more persuasive, we hold today that a plaintiff need not plead expressly the capacity in which he is suing a defendant in order to state a cause of action under § 1983"). *See also* Rodriguez v. Phillips, 66 F.3d 470, 482 (2d Cir. 1995) ("Where, as here, doubt may exist as to whether an official is sued personally, in his official capacity or in both capacities, the course of proceedings ordinarily resolves the nature of the liability sought to be imposed.").

316. *See, e.g.,* Leach v. Shelby County Sheriff, 891 F.2d 1241, 1245 (6th Cir. 1989), *cert. denied*, 495 U.S. 932 (1990).

317. *See infra* Chapter 7.

fendant has no qualified immunity from compensatory damages liability.[318]

Pleading Requirement

In *Leatherman v. Tarrant County Narcotics Intelligence & Coordination Unit,*[319] the Supreme Court unanimously rejected the "heightened pleading standard" in cases alleging municipal liability. The Court held that the lower court had erroneously upheld the dismissal of a complaint against a governmental entity for failure to plead with the requisite specificity.[320] While leaving open the question of "whether our qualified immunity jurisprudence would require a heightened pleading in cases involving individual government officials,"[321] the Supreme Court refused to equate a municipality's freedom from *respondeat superior* liability with immunity from suit.[322] Finding it "impossible to square the 'heightened pleading requirement' . . . with the liberal system of 'notice pleading' set up by the Federal Rules[,]" the Court suggested that Federal Rules 8 and 9(b) would have to be rewritten to incorporate such a "heightened pleading standard."[323] The Court concluded by noting that "[i]n the absence of such an amendment, federal courts and litigants must rely on summary judgment and control of discovery to weed out unmeritorious claims sooner rather than later."[324]

---

318. Owen v. City of Independence, 445 U.S. 622 (1980). On the other hand, while punitive damages may be awarded against individual defendants under § 1983 (*see* Smith v. Wade, 461 U.S. 30 (1983)), local governments are absolutely immune from punitive damages. City of Newport v. Fact Concerts, Inc., 453 U.S. 247 (1981).

319. 113 S. Ct. 1160 (1993).

320. Leatherman v. Tarrant County Narcotics Intelligence & Coordination Unit, 954 F.2d 1054, 1058 (5th Cir. 1992).

321. *Leatherman,* 113 S. Ct. at 1162.

322. *Id.*

323. *Id.* at 1163.

324. *Id.* For post-*Leatherman* decisions involving pleading against local government entities, see *Atchinson v. District of Columbia,* 73 F.3d 418, 423 (D.C. Cir. 1996) ("A complaint describing a single instance of official misconduct and alleging a failure to train may put a municipality on notice of the nature and basis of a plaintiff's claim."); *Jordan v. Jackson,* 15 F.3d 333, 339 (4th Cir. 1994) ("We believe it is clear . . . that the Supreme Court's rejection of the Fifth Circuit's 'heightened pleading standard' in *Leatherman* constitutes a rejection of the specific requirement that a plaintiff plead multiple instances of similar constitutional violations to support an allegation of municipal policy or custom.").

Methods of Establishing Municipal Liability

Unconstitutional Policy

The clearest case for government liability under *Monell v. Department of Social Services*[325] is a case like *Monell* itself, where an unconstitutional policy statement, ordinance, regulation, or decision is formally adopted and promulgated by the governing body itself or a department or agency thereof. In *Monell*, the Department of Social Services and the Board of Education had officially adopted a policy requiring pregnant employees to take unpaid maternity leave before medically necessary.[326]

The challenged policy statement, ordinance, regulation, or decision must have been adopted or promulgated by the local entity. A local government's *mere enforcement* of state law, as opposed to express incorporation or adoption of state law into local regulations or codes, has been found insufficient to establish *Monell* liability.[327]

"Custom or Usage"

Monell allows the imposition of government liability not only when the challenged conduct executes or implements a formally adopted policy, but also when that conduct reflects "practices of state officials so permanent and well settled as to constitute a 'custom or usage' with the force of law."[328] Liability is attributed to the municipality in custom-type cases

---

325. 436 U.S. 658 (1978).

326. *See also* City of Newport v. Fact Concerts, Inc., 453 U.S. 247 (1981) (vote of City Council to cancel license for rock concert was official decision for *Monell* purposes); Owen v. City of Independence, 445 U.S. 622 (1980) (personnel decision made by City Council constitutes official city policy). Note that in both *Fact Concerts* and *Owen*, decisions officially adopted by the government body itself need not have general or recurring application in order to constitute official "policy."

327. *See, e.g.*, Surplus Store & Exchange, Inc. v. City of Delphi, 928 F.2d 788, 793 (7th Cir. 1991). *But see* McKusick v. City of Melbourne, 96 F.3d 478, 484 (11th Cir. 1996) (holding that development and implementation of administrative enforcement procedure, going beyond terms of state court injunction, leading to arrest of all antiabortion protesters found within buffer zone, including persons not named in injunction, amounted to cognizable policy choice); Garner v. Memphis Police Dep't, 8 F.3d 358, 364 (6th Cir. 1993) (rejecting defendants' argument that they had no choice but to follow state "fleeing felon" policy, holding that "[d]efendants' decision to authorize use of deadly force to apprehend nondangerous fleeing burglary suspects was . . . a deliberate choice from among various alternatives. . . ."), *cert. denied*, 114 S. Ct. 1219 (1994).

328. *Monell*, 436 U.S. at 691. *See also* Bouman v. Block, 940 F.2d 1211 (9th Cir. 1991)

through a policy maker's actual or constructive knowledge of and acquiescence in the unconstitutional custom or practice.[329] Acts of omission, as well as commission, may serve as the predicate for a finding of unconstitutional policy or custom.[330]

Failure to Train, Supervise, or Discipline

A city may be liable for failure to train, supervise, or discipline its employees. In *City of Oklahoma City v. Tuttle*,[331] seven justices agreed that a verdict against the city could not be upheld where the trial court had instructed the jury that "a single, unusually excessive use of force [by a police officer] may . . . warrant an inference that it was attributable to inadequate training or supervision amounting to 'deliberate indifference' or 'gross negligence' on the part of the officials in charge."[332] However, the only clear consensus reached in *Tuttle* was that municipal liability based on a policy of inadequate training could not be derived from a single incident of misconduct by a non-policy-making municipal employee.

In *City of Canton v. Harris*,[333] the Court unanimously rejected the city's argument that municipal liability can be imposed only where the

("If a practice is so permanent and well settled as to constitute a 'custom or usage' with the force of law, a plaintiff may proceed . . . despite the absence of written authorization or express municipal policy."), *cert. denied*, 112 S. Ct. 640 (1992).

329. *See, e.g.*, McNabola v. Chicago Transit Auth., 10 F.3d 501, 511 (7th Cir. 1993) ("A municipal 'custom' may be established by proof of the knowledge of policymaking officials and their acquiescence in the established practice.").

330. *See, e.g.*, Oviatt v. Pearce, 954 F.2d 1470, 1477 (9th Cir. 1992) (holding that "[t]he decision not to take any action to alleviate the problem of detecting missed arraignments constitutes a policy for purposes of § 1983 municipal liability").

331. 471 U.S. 808 (1985).

332. *Id.* at 813.

333. 489 U.S. 378 (1989). In *City of Canton*, the plaintiff claimed a deprivation of her right, under the due process clause, to receive necessary medical care while in police custody. She asserted a claim of municipal liability for this deprivation based on a theory of "grossly inadequate training." The plaintiff presented evidence of a municipal regulation, establishing a policy of giving police shift commanders complete discretion to make decisions as to whether prisoners were in need of medical care, accompanied by evidence that such commanders received no training or guidelines to assist in making such judgments. *Id.* at 382. The Sixth Circuit upheld the adequacy of the district court's jury instructions on the issue of municipal liability for inadequate training, stating that the plaintiff could succeed on her failure-to-train claim "[where] the plaintiff . . . prove[s] that the municipality acted recklessly, intentionally, or with gross negligence." *Id.* (quoting App. to Pet. for Cert. at 5a).

challenged policy is itself unconstitutional, and concluded that "there are limited circumstances in which an allegation of a 'failure to train' can be the basis for liability under § 1983."[334] The Court held that "the inadequacy of training policy may serve as the basis for § 1983 liability only where the failure to train amounts to deliberate indifference to the rights of persons with whom the police come into contact."[335]

The Court was careful to note that the "deliberate indifference" standard has nothing to do with the level of culpability that may be required to make out the underlying constitutional wrong, but rather has to do with what is required to establish the municipal policy as the "moving force" behind the constitutional violation.[336] On remand the plaintiff would have to identify a particular deficiency in the training program and prove that the identified deficiency was the actual cause of the plaintiff's constitutional injury. It would not be enough to establish that the particular officer was inadequately trained, nor that there was negligent administration of an otherwise adequate program, nor that the conduct resulting in the injury could have been avoided by more or better training. The federal courts are not to become involved "in an endless exercise of second-guessing municipal employee-training programs."[337]

---

334. *Id.* at 387.

335. *Id.* at 388. The Court observed that:

> [I]t may happen that in light of the duties assigned to specific officers or employees the need for more or different training is so obvious, and the inadequacy so likely to result in the violation of constitutional rights, that the policymakers of the city can reasonably be said to have been deliberately indifferent to the need. In that event, the failure to provide proper training may fairly be said to represent a policy for which the city is responsible, and for which the city may be held liable if it actually causes injury. [footnotes omitted]

Id. at 390.

336. *Id.* at 388 n.8. In *Farmer v. Brennan*, 114 S. Ct. 1970 (1994), the Supreme Court recognized two types of deliberate indifference: subjective deliberate indifference and objective deliberate indifference. Subjective deliberate indifference is necessary to prove an Eighth Amendment violation by prison officials. *Id.* at 1980. "[A] prison official may be held liable under the Eighth Amendment for denying humane conditions of confinement only if he knows that inmates face a substantial risk of serious harm and disregards that risk by failing to take reasonable measures to abate it." *Id.* at 1984. In contrast, objective deliberate indifference is necessary to prove a failure-to-train case. "It would be hard to describe the *Canton* understanding of deliberate indifference, permitting liability to be premised on obviousness or constructive notice, as anything but objective." *Id.* at 1981.

337. *City of Canton*, 489 U.S. at 390–91.

Justice Sandra Day O'Connor, in her concurring opinion, elaborated on how a plaintiff could show that a municipality was deliberately indifferent to an obvious need for training. First, where there is "a clear constitutional duty implicated in recurrent situations that a particular employee is certain to face, . . . failure to inform city personnel of that duty will create an extremely high risk that constitutional violations will ensue."[338]

Justice O'Connor was also willing to recognize that municipal liability on a "failure to train" theory might be established "where it can be shown that policy makers were aware of, and acquiesced in, a pattern of constitutional violations involving the exercise of police discretion, . . . [which pattern] could put the municipality on notice that its officers confront the particular situations on a regular basis, and that they often react in a manner contrary to constitutional requirements."[339]

Thus, *City of Canton* identifies two different approaches to a failure-to-train case.[340] First, deliberate indifference may be established by demonstrating a failure to train officials in a specific area where there is an obvious need for training in order to avoid violations of citizens' constitutional rights.[341] Second, a municipality may be held responsible under

338. *Id.* at 396 (O'Connor, J., concurring in part and dissenting in part). For example, all of the Justices agreed that there is an obvious need to train police officers as to the constitutional limitations on the use of deadly force (*see* Tennessee v. Garner, 471 U.S. 1 (1985)), and that a failure to so train would be so certain to result in constitutional violations as to reflect the "deliberate indifference" to constitutional rights required for the imposition of municipal liability. *Id.* at 390 n.10.

339. *Id.* at 397 (O'Connor, J., concurring in part and dissenting in part).

340. *See, e.g.,* Cornfield v. Consolidated High Sch. Dist. No. 230, 991 F.2d 1316, 1327 (7th Cir. 1993) (setting out an analysis which clearly illustrates the two different methods of establishing *City of Canton* deliberate indifference); Thelma D. v. Board of Educ., 934 F.2d 929, 934–45 (8th Cir. 1991) (same).

341. For examples of cases in which courts have found a failure to train in an area where the need for training is obvious, see, e.g., *Allen v. Muskogee*, 119 F.3d 837, 843 (10th Cir. 1997) (finding need for different training obvious where "[c]ity trained its officers to leave cover and approach armed suicidal, emotionally disturbed persons and to try to disarm them, a practice contrary to proper police procedures and tactical principles"); *Zuchel v. City & County of Denver*, 997 F.2d 730, 741 (10th Cir. 1993) (finding evidence clearly sufficient to permit jury reasonably to infer that Denver's failure to implement recommended periodic live "shoot—don't shoot" range training constituted deliberate indifference to the constitutional rights of Denver citizens); *Davis v. Mason County*, 927 F.2d 1473, 1483 (9th Cir. 1991) ("Mason County's failure to train its officers in the legal limits of the use of force constituted 'deliberate indifference' to the safety of its inhabi-

§ 1983 where a pattern of unconstitutional conduct is so pervasive as to imply actual or constructive knowledge of the conduct on the part of policy makers, whose deliberate indifference to the unconstitutional practice is evidenced by a failure to correct the situation once the need for training became obvious.[342]

Under some circumstances, having no policy may constitute deliberate indifference.[343] Furthermore, at least one court of appeals has rejected the notion "that a municipality may shield itself from liability for failure to train its police officers in a given area simply by offering a course nominally covering the subject, regardless of how substandard the content and quality of that training is."[344]

Failure to Screen in Hiring

In *Board of County Commissioners v. Brown*,[345] the Supreme Court revisited the issue of municipal liability under § 1983 in the context of a single bad hiring decision made by a county sheriff who was stipulated to be the final policy maker for the county in matters of law enforcement.

Sheriff B.J. Moore hired his son's nephew, Stacy Burns, despite an extensive "rap sheet" that included numerous violations and arrests but no felonies. The plaintiff suffered a severe knee injury when Reserve Deputy Burns forcibly extracted her from the car driven by her husband, who

tants as a matter of law."), *cert. denied*, 112 S. Ct. 275 (1991).

342. *See, e.g.*, Chew v. Gates, 27 F.3d 1432, 1445 (9th Cir. 1994) ("Where the city equips its police officers with potentially dangerous animals, and evidence is adduced that those animals inflict injury in a significant percentage of the cases in which they are used, a failure to adopt a departmental policy governing their use, or to implement rules or regulations regarding the constitutional limits of that use, evidences a 'deliberate indifference' to constitutional rights.").

343. *See, e.g.*, Vineyard v. County of Murray, 990 F.2d 1207, 1212 (11th Cir. 1993) ("The evidence demonstrates that the Sheriff's Department had inadequate procedures for recording and following up complaints against individual officers . . . no policies and procedures manual . . . [and] inadequate policies of supervision, discipline and training of deputies in the Murray County Sheriff's Department. . . ."); Oviatt v. Pearce, 954 F.2d 1470, 1477–78 (9th Cir. 1992) (holding that the decision not to take any action to alleviate the problem of detecting missed arraignments constitutes a policy of deliberate indifference to the obvious likelihood of prolonged and unjustified incarcerations).

344. Russo v. City of Cincinnati, 953 F.2d 1036, 1047 (6th Cir. 1992) (finding that the simple fact that officers took a seven-hour course entitled "Disturbed-Distressed Persons" did not mean that their training was adequate as a matter of law).

345. 117 S. Ct. 1382 (1997).

had avoided a police checkpoint. She sued both Burns and the county under § 1983.

In a five–four opinion written by Justice O'Connor, the Supreme Court held that the county did not violate the plaintiff's rights by hiring Deputy Burns.[346] It distinguished Brown's claim, involving a single lawful hiring decision that ultimately resulted in a constitutional violation, from a claim that "a particular municipal action itself violates federal law, or directs an employee to do so."[347] As the Court noted, its prior cases recognizing municipal liability based on a single act or decision attributed to the government entity involved decisions of local legislative bodies or policy makers that directly effected or ordered someone to effect a constitutional deprivation.[348] The majority also rejected the plaintiff's effort to analogize inadequate screening to a failure to train.[349]

The majority insisted on evidence from which a jury could find that, had Sheriff Moore adequately screened Deputy Burns' background, he "should have concluded that Burns' use of excessive force would be a plainly obvious consequence of the hiring decision."[350] In the view of the majority, scrutiny of Burns' record did not produce sufficient evidence from which a jury could make such a finding.[351]

346. *Id.* at 1393.

347. *Id.* at 1388.

348. *See, e.g.,* Pembaur v. City of Cincinnati, 475 U.S. 469 (1986) (county prosecutor gave order that resulted in constitutional violation); City of Newport v. Fact Concerts, Inc., 453 U.S. 247 (1981) (decision of city council to cancel license permitting concert directly violated constitutional rights); Owen v. City of Independence, 445 U.S. 622 (1980) (city council discharged employee without due process). In such cases, there are no real problems with respect to the issues of fault or causation. *See also* Bennett v. Pippin, 74 F.3d 578, 586 & n.5 (5th Cir. 1996) (holding county liable for sheriff's rape of murder suspect, where sheriff was final policy maker in matters of law enforcement).

349. *Brown,* 117 S. Ct. at 1391.

350. *Id.* at 1392.

351. *Id.* at 1393. It is somewhat early to predict what impact *Brown* will have on municipal liability cases. For post-*Brown* decisions, *see, e.g., Allen v. Muskogee,* 119 F.3d 837, 845 (10th Cir. 1997) ("The case before us is within the 'narrow range of circumstances' recognized by *Canton* and left intact by *Brown,* under which a single violation of federal rights may be a highly predictable consequence of failure to train officers to handle recurring situations with an obvious potential for such a violation. The likelihood that officers will frequently have to deal with armed emotionally upset persons, and the predictability that officers trained to leave cover, approach, and attempt to disarm such persons will provoke a violent response, could justify a finding that the City's failure to properly train its officers reflected deliberate indifference to the obvious consequence of the City's

Justice Souter, joined by Justices Breyer and Stevens, dissented, characterizing the majority opinion as an expression of "deep skepticism" that "converts a newly-demanding formulation of the standard of fault into a virtually categorical impossibility of showing it in a case like this."[352]

Justice Stephen G. Breyer, joined by Justices Ginsburg and Stevens, criticized the "highly complex body of interpretive law" that has developed to maintain and perpetuate the distinction adopted in *Monell* between direct and vicarious liability, and calls for a reexamination of "the legal soundness of that basic distinction itself."[353]

Conduct of Policy-Making Officials Attributed to Governmental Entity

Under *Monell*, government liability attaches when the constitutional injury results from the implementation or "execution of a government's policy or custom, whether made by its lawmakers *or by those whose edicts or acts may fairly be said to represent official policy*."[354] Since *Monell*, the Court has struggled with the questions left open by that decision. In subsequent cases, there have been attempts to clarify the important issues of (1) whose "edicts or acts," beyond those of the official lawmakers, may be attributed to the government, and (2) which "edicts or acts" will constitute "policy."

---

choice. The likelihood of a violent response to this type of police action also may support an inference of causation—that the City's indifference led directly to the very consequence that was so predictable."); *Doe v. Hillsboro Independent School District*, 113 F.3d 1412, 1416 (5th Cir. 1997) (en banc) ("When the district court afforded Doe the opportunity to amend his complaint, he could not even allege that the custodian who assaulted his daughter either had a prior record of violent crime or previously had been reported to the officials for sexual misbehavior towards students. Even in the context of resisting a Rule 12 motion to dismiss, plaintiffs have demonstrated an inability to show a nexus between any failure to check criminal background and this assault.").

352. *Brown*, 117 S. Ct. at 1396 (Souter, J., joined by Stevens and Breyer, JJ., dissenting).

353. *Id.* at 1401 (Breyer, J., joined by Stevens and Ginsburg, JJ., dissenting). One of our authors was among those who first criticized the rejection of respondeat superior liability in *Monell*. See Karen M. Blum, *From* Monroe *to* Monell: *Defining the Scope of Municipal Liability in Federal Courts*, 51 Temple L.Q. 409 (1978), *cited in Pembaur v. City of Cincinnati*, 475 U.S. 469, 489 n.4 (1986) (Stevens, J., concurring in part and concurring in judgment).

354. Monell v. Department of Soc. Servs., 436 U.S. 658, 694 (1978) (emphasis added).

In *Pembaur v. City of Cincinnati,*[355] a majority of the Court held that a single decision by an official with policy-making authority in a given area could constitute official policy and be attributed to the government itself under certain circumstances.[356] The county prosecutor ordered local law enforcement officers to "go in and get" two witnesses who were believed to be inside the clinic of their employer, a doctor who had been indicted for fraud with respect to government payments for medical care provided to welfare recipients. The officers had capiases for the arrest of the witnesses, but no search warrant for the premises of the clinic. Pursuant to the county prosecutor's order, they broke down the door and searched the clinic.[357]

In holding that the county could be held liable for this single decision by the county prosecutor who ordered the violation of the plaintiff's constitutional rights, the Court described the "appropriate circumstances" in which a single decision by policy makers may give rise to municipal liability. For example, the Court noted cases in which it had held that a single decision by a "properly constituted legislative body . . . constitute[d] an act of official government policy."[358] But *Monell's* language encompasses other officials "whose acts or edicts" could constitute official policy.[359] Thus, where a government's authorized decision maker adopts a particular course of action, the government may be responsible

---

355. 475 U.S. 469 (1986).

356. Justice White wrote separately to make clear his position (concurred in by Justice O'Connor) that a decision of a policy-making official could not result in municipal liability if that decision were contrary to controlling federal, state, or local law. *Pembaur*, 475 U.S. at 485–87 (White, J., concurring). Since the law was not settled at the time of the county prosecutor's action in *Pembaur*, the decision of the policy-making official would constitute the official policy for *Monell* purposes.

Justice Powell (joined by Chief Justice Burger and Justice Rehnquist) dissented, criticizing the Court for its focus upon the "status of the decisionmaker" rather than "the nature of the decision reached . . . and . . . the process by which the decision was reached." *Id.* at 492–502 (Powell, J., dissenting).

357. *Id.* at 472, 473.

358. *Id.* at 480 (citing Owen v. City of Independence, 445 U.S. 622 (1980) (City Council passed resolution firing plaintiff without a pretermination hearing) and City of Newport v. Fact Concerts, Inc., 453 U.S. 247 (1981) (city council canceled license permitting concert because of dispute over content of performance)).

359. *Id.* (citing *Monell*, 436 U.S. at 694).

for that policy "whether that action is to be taken only once or to be taken repeatedly."[360]

Justice William J. Brennan, Jr., writing for a plurality in *Pembaur*, concluded that "[m]un icipal liability attaches only where the decision-maker possesses final authority to establish municipal policy with respect to the action ordered."[361] Whether an official possesses policy-making authority with respect to particular matters will be determined by state law. Policy-making authority may be bestowed by legislative enactment or delegated by an official possessing such authority under state law.[362]

In *City of St. Louis v. Praprotnik*,[363] the Court made another attempt "to determin[e] when isolated decisions by municipal officials or employees may expose the municipality itself to liability under [section] 1983."[364] Justice O'Connor, writing for a plurality, reinforced the principle articulated in *Pembaur* that state law will be used to determine policy-making status.[365] Furthermore, identifying a policy-making official is a question of law, for the court to decide by reference to state law, not one of fact to be submitted to a jury.[366] The plurality also underscored the

360. *Id*. at 481.

361. *Id.*

362. *Id.* at 483.

363. 485 U.S. 112 (1988).

364. *Id.* at 113. The Court reversed a decision by the Eighth Circuit Court of Appeals which had found the city liable for the transfer and layoff of a city architect in violation of his First Amendment rights. The court of appeals had allowed the plaintiff to attribute to the city adverse personnel decisions made by the plaintiff's supervisors where such decisions were considered "final" because they were not subject to *de novo* review by higher-ranking officials. City of St. Louis v. Praprotnik, 798 F.2d 1168, 1173–75 (8th Cir. 1986).

365. *Id.* at 124.

366. *Id.* In *Praprotnik*, the relevant law was found in the St. Louis City Charter, which gave policy-making authority in matters of personnel to the mayor, aldermen, and Civil Service Commission. *Id*. at 126. *See also* Dotson v. Chester, 937 F.2d 920 (4th Cir. 1991) (court examines state law and county code to find Sheriff final policy maker as to operation of county jail).

In *Jett v. Dallas Independent School District,* 491 U.S. 701 (1989), the Court stressed that the identification of final policy-making authority is "a legal question to be resolved by the trial judge *before* the case is submitted to the jury." *Id*. at 737 (emphasis in original). The Court also underscored the "relevant legal materials" to be reviewed by the trial judge in identifying official policy makers, including "'custom or usage' having the force of law." *Id*. (quoting *Praprotnik*, 485 U.S. at 124 n.1). Once the court has identified the policy makers in the given area, "it is for the jury to determine whether *their* decisions have caused the deprivation of rights at issue by policies which affirmatively command

importance of "finality" to the concept of policy making and reiterated the distinction set out in *Pembaur* between authority to make final policy and authority to make discretionary decisions. "When an official's discretionary decisions are constrained by policies not of that official's making, those policies, rather than the subordinate's departures from them, are the act of the municipality."[367] Finally, the plurality noted that for a subordinate's decision to be attributable to the government entity, "the authorized policymakers [must] approve [the] decision and the basis for it. . . . Simply going along with discretionary decisions made by one's subordinates . . . is not a delegation to them of authority to make policy."[368]

Supervisory Liability

It is important not to confuse the concept of municipal liability for failure to supervise with the concept of supervisory liability. Supervisory liability can be imposed without a determination of municipal liability. Supervisory liability runs against the individual, is based on his or her personal responsibility for the constitutional violation, and does not require any proof of official policy or custom as the "moving force" behind the conduct.

"[W]hen supervisory liability is imposed, it is imposed against the supervisory official in his individual capacity for his own culpable action or inaction in the training, supervision, or control of his subordinates."[369] As with a local government defendant, a supervisor cannot be held liable under § 1983 on a *respondeat superior* basis,[370] although a supervisory official may be liable even where not directly involved in the constitutional

that it occur . . . or by acquiescence in a longstanding practice or custom which constitutes the 'standard operating procedure' of the local governmental entity." *Jett,* 491 U.S. at 737 (emphasis in original).

367. *Praprotnik,* 485 U.S. at 127. *See, e.g.,* Auriemma v. Rice, 957 F.2d 397, 400 (7th Cir. 1992) ("Liability for unauthorized acts is personal; to hold the municipality liable . . . the agent's action must implement rather than frustrate the government's policy.").

368. *Praprotnik,* 485 U.S. at 129–30. *See, e.g.,* Gillette v. Delmore, 979 F.2d 1342, 1348 (9th Cir. 1992) (concluding that mere inaction on part of policy maker "does not amount to 'ratification' under *Pembaur* and *Praprotnik*").

369. Clay v. Conlee, 815 F.2d 1164, 1170 (8th Cir. 1987).

370. Monell v. Department of Soc. Servs., 436 U.S. 658, 694 n.58 (1978).

violation.[371] The misconduct of the subordinate must be "affirmatively link[ed]" to the action or inaction of the supervisor.[372]

Since supervisory liability based on inaction is separate and distinct from the liability imposed on the subordinate employees for the underlying constitutional violation, the level of culpability that must be alleged to make out the supervisor's liability may not be the same as the level of culpability mandated by the particular constitutional right involved. While § 1983 itself contains no independent state of mind requirement,[373] federal appellate courts consistently require plaintiffs to show something more than mere negligence, yet less than actual intent in order to establish supervisory liability.[374]

A number of circuits use the Supreme Court's analysis in *City of Canton v. Harris*[375] as an analogy in determining whether a supervisory official is deliberately indifferent to the violation of constitutional rights. In *Shaw v. Stroud*,[376] the court held that a three-prong test must be applied in determining a supervisor's liability. A plaintiff must establish:

(1) that the supervisor had actual or constructive knowledge that his subordinate was engaged in conduct that posed "a pervasive and unreasonable risk" of constitutional injury to citizens like the plaintiff; (2) that the supervisor's response to that knowledge was so inadequate as to show "deliberate indifference to or tacit authorization of the alleged offensive practices"; and (3) that there was an "affirmative causal link"

---

371. Wilks v. Young, 897 F.2d 896, 898 (7th Cir. 1990).

372. Rizzo v. Goode, 423 U.S. 362, 371 (1976).

373. Parratt v. Taylor, 451 U.S. 527, 535 (1981), *overruled in part on other grounds*, Daniels v. Williams, 474 U.S. 327 (1986).

374. *See, e.g.*, Lankford v. City of Hobart, 73 F.3d 283, 287 (10th Cir. 1996) (following Third Circuit approach, which requires personal direction or actual knowledge for supervisory liability); Baker v. Monroe Township, 50 F.3d 1186, 1194 & n.5 (3d Cir. 1995) (applying Third Circuit standard, which requires "actual knowledge and acquiescence" and noting that other circuits have broader standards for supervisory liability); Howard v. Adkison, 887 F.2d 134, 138 (8th Cir. 1989) (holding that evidence was sufficient to allow the jury to find supervisors' inaction amounted to reckless disregard of constitutional violations); Gutierrez-Rodriguez v. Cartagena, 882 F.2d 553, 562 (1st Cir. 1989) (stating that supervisor's conduct or inaction must be shown to amount to a reckless or callous indifference to the constitutional rights of others).

375. 489 U.S. 378 (1989).

376. 13 F.3d 791 (4th Cir. 1994).

between the supervisor's inaction and the particular constitutional injury suffered by the plaintiff.[377]

Although the courts do not differ significantly as to the level of culpability required for supervisory liability, there is some split on the question of whether the requisite culpability for supervisory inaction can be established on the basis of a single incident of subordinates' misconduct or whether a pattern or practice of constitutional violations must be shown.[378]

377. *Id.* at 798 (quoting Miltier v. Beorn, 896 F.2d 848, 854 (4th Cir. 1990)), *cert. denied*, 513 U.S. 814 (1994); *see also* Doe v. Taylor Indep. Sch. Dist., 15 F.3d 443, 453 (5th Cir. 1994) (en banc) ("The most significant difference between *City of Canton* and this case is that the former dealt with a municipality's liability whereas the latter deals with an individual supervisor's liability. The legal elements of an individual's supervisory liability and a political subdivision's liability, however, are similar enough that the same standards of fault and causation should govern."), *cert. denied sub nom.* Lankford v. Doe, 115 S. Ct. 70 (1994); Greason v. Kemp, 891 F.2d 829, 836–37 (11th Cir. 1990) (finding *City of Canton* analysis a helpful analogy in determining whether a supervisory official was deliberately indifferent to an inmate's psychiatric needs).

378. *Compare* Howard v. Adkison, 887 F.2d 134, 138 (8th Cir. 1989) ("A single incident, or a series of isolated incidents, usually provides an insufficient basis upon which to assign supervisory liability.") *with* Gutierrez-Rodriguez v. Cartagena, 882 F.2d 553, 567 (1st Cir. 1989) ("An inquiry into whether there has been a pattern of past abuses or official condonation thereof is only required when a plaintiff has sued a municipality. Where . . . plaintiff has brought suit against the defendants as individuals . . . plaintiff need only establish that the defendants' acts or omissions were the product of reckless or callous indifference to his constitutional rights and that they, in fact, caused his constitutional deprivations.").

Chapter 6
Absolute Immunity: A Functional Approach

If the challenged action by a state official is a judicial, quasi-judicial, prosecutorial, or legislative function, absolute immunity shields the official from having to pay damages for the alleged constitutional violation. As an affirmative defense, absolute immunity applies only when a governmental official performs one of these functions. The immunity does not attach to the office, but rather to certain functions performed by the official. With respect to legislative acts, absolute immunity bars both injunctive and monetary relief; with respect to judicial acts, Congress amended § 1983 to prohibit injunctive relief unless "declaratory relief was violated" or unavailable. Except for these circumstances, absolute immunity does not bar injunctive relief. This potent defense applies even when officials maliciously violated a plaintiff's constitutional rights.[379]

Although the statute on its face does not refer to any immunity, the Supreme Court has recognized both absolute and qualified immunity as a defense by ascertaining Congress's intent to provide immunities. In doing so, the Court has stated that "[m]ost officials are entitled only to qualified immunity."[380] It has limited application of the absolute immunity defense by applying a two-part standard. First, the Court considers whether the common law recognized an immunity. Second, if it did, then the Court questions whether the history or purpose of § 1983 supports applying the common-law immunity. Even if Congress intended absolute immunity to apply to a given function, courts must nevertheless question

---

379. *See, e.g.,* Pierson v. Ray, 386 U.S. 547, 553–54 (1967).
380. Buckley v. Fitzsimmons, 113 S. Ct. 2606, 2613 (1993).

whether the challenged action was legislative, judicial, quasi-judicial, or prosecutorial.

Legislative Functions

When officials perform legislative functions, they receive the broadest relief available under § 1983 because, in this unique context, absolute immunity bars both injunctive relief and damage awards. In *Tenny v. Brandhove*,[381] the Supreme Court held that state legislators performed protected legislative functions when they served on investigative committees.[382] The Court explained, "Investigations, whether by standing or special committees, are an established part of representative government."[383] Unable and unwilling to saddle legislators with liability for this investigative function, the Court found that the legislators' self-discipline and the voters' ability not to reelect legislators were adequate checks on abuse of legislative power.

Other officials can also perform legislative acts. In *Lake Country Estates, Inc. v. Tahoe Regional Planning Agency* (TRPA),[384] the Court determined that the TRPA's decision regarding land use was a legislative act. TRPA was an agency created by the states of California and Nevada, with the approval of Congress, with the agency's purpose being to create a regional plan for "land use, transportation, conservation, recreation, and public services."[385] The Court held that absolute immunity applied, even though there was no common-law immunity for such an entity and even though all the members of the agency were appointed, not elected.

The most difficult issue in determining whether absolute immunity applies is whether the challenged action was legislative, rather than administrative or executive.[386] In *Supreme Court of Virginia v. Consumers Union of the United States*,[387] the Court determined that the justices of

---

381. 341 U.S. 367, 379 (1951).

382. *Id.* at 379.

383. *Id.* at 377.

384. 440 U.S. 391 (1979).

385. *Id.* at 394.

386. *See, e.g.*, Yeldell v. Cooper Green Hosp., 956 F.2d 1056, 1063 (11th Cir. 1992) (decision not to introduce legislation was a legislative act); Cinevision Corp. v. City of Burbank, 745 F.2d 560 (9th Cir. 1984), *cert. denied*, 471 U.S. 1054 (1985) (administering municipal contracts was an executive function).

387. 446 U.S. 719, 731–34 (1980).

the Virginia Supreme Court had performed a legislative act in promulgating professional responsibility rules for attorneys.[388] The Court stated that the Virginia court had exercised "the State's entire legislative power with respect to regulating the bar[,] and its members are the State's legislators for the purpose of issuing" the rules.[389] By focusing on the action performed, not the job description of the actor, the Court emphasized the functional nature of absolute immunity.

In *Bogan v. Scott-Harris*,[390] the Supreme Court held that local legislators are entitled to absolute immunity for their legislative activities.[391] The Court unanimously decided to extend absolute immunity to a city council member and mayor, whose challenged actions were promulgating a new city budget and signing a law that eliminated the plaintiff's position, after she had complained about racial epithets in the workplace.

Judicial Acts

Judicial acts are also protected by absolute immunity. In several decisions, the Supreme Court has broadly defined judicial actions.

In *Pierson v. Ray*,[392] the Court held that the judicial functions of determining guilt and sentencing a criminal defendant are protected by absolute immunity.[393] Such immunity is proper for two reasons: the common law of 1871 supported immunity, and the policy behind § 1983 was not to deter judges from performing their jobs:

> [I]mmunity is not for the protection or benefit of a malicious or corrupt judge, but for the benefit of the public, whose interest it is that the judges should be at liberty to exercise their functions with independence and without fear of consequences. It is a judge's duty to decide all cases within his jurisdiction that are brought before him, including controversial cases that arouse the most intense feelings in the litigants. His errors may be corrected on appeal, but he should not have to fear that unsatisfied litigants may hound him with litigation charging malice

---

388. *Id.* at 731–34.
389. *Id.* at 734.
390. 118 S. Ct. 966 (1998).
391. *Id.* at 972.
392. 386 U.S. 547 (1967).
393. *Id.* at 554–55.

or corruption. Imposing such a burden on judges would contribute not to principled and fearless decision-making but to intimidation.[394]

In short, absolute immunity is necessary to protect the judicial system. The remedy for judicial errors is an appeal, not a § 1983 lawsuit for damages.

Subsequently the Court had to define the boundaries of "judicial" actions. In *Stump v. Sparkman*,[395] the Court held that Judge Harold D. Stump had performed a judicial act when he ordered a mentally retarded girl to undergo a tubal ligation at the request of her mother.[396] The Court explained that absolute immunity applies to actions taken by judges "in excess of [their] authority," but not in the "clear absence of all jurisdiction."[397] To distinguish between these two standards, the Court provided an example: If a probate judge who has jurisdiction only over wills nevertheless tries a criminal case, then the judge has acted in the "clear absence of jurisdiction." On the other hand, if a judge with jurisdiction over criminal matters convicts a defendant of a nonexistent crime, then the judge has performed a "judicial act" in "excess of his jurisdiction."[398]

Furthermore, an action can be judicial even if it lacks the formality often associated with court proceedings. In determining whether an act is judicial, the question is whether the action is one normally performed by a judge. For example, in *Stump* the Court recognized absolute immunity for the judge's act of ordering a tubal ligation, even though there had been no docket number, no filing with the clerk's office, and no notice to the minor. Similarly, in *Mireles v. Waco*,[399] the Court held that a judge had performed a judicial act in ordering a bailiff to use excessive force to compel an attorney to attend court proceedings.[400] Even though judges do not have the authority to order police officers to commit a battery, they nevertheless have broad authority to maintain court proceedings.

---

394. *Id.* at 553–54.
395. 435 U.S. 349, 364 (1978).
396. *Id.* at 364.
397. *Id.* at 356–57.
398. *Id.* at 357 n.7.
399. 502 U.S. 9 (1991).
400. *Id.* at 13.

Distinguishing Judicial and Quasi-Judicial Functions from Administrative Acts

Not all actions by judges may be protected by absolute immunity. Administrative functions are protected only by qualified immunity. In *Forrester v. White*,[401] the Supreme Court held that when a judge fired a probation officer, he performed an administrative act, protected only by qualified immunity.[402] The Court rejected the argument that judges should have absolute immunity for employment decisions because an incompetent employee can impair the judge's ability to make sound judicial decisions. The Court also noted that because judges are less able to delegate decision making there is less reason to afford them absolute immunity in contrast to other officials.

Because of the functional nature of absolute immunity, many officials have attempted to assert absolute immunity for quasi-judicial functions. Although the Court rejected a court reporter's claim for absolute immunity for her failure to timely produce a transcript for an appeal,[403] the Court granted absolute immunity for decisions made by a judge at an administrative hearing.[404] In contrast, both prison officials and school board members may assert only qualified immunity for their decisions to punish. The Court in *Cleavinger v. Saxner*[405] held that a committee of prison officials did not perform a judicial act in deciding to discipline a prisoner after a hearing.[406] Noting that the committee members were not administrative law judges, the Court characterized them as employees "temporarily diverted from their usual duties." Similarly in *Wood v. Strickland*,[407] the Court held that absolute immunity was not necessary to protect school board members' ability to exercise discretion in deciding how to discipline students.[408]

---

401. 484 U.S. 219 (1988).
402. *Id.* at 230.
403. Antoine v. Byers & Anderson, Inc., 508 U.S. 429, 437 (1993).
404. Butz v. Economou, 438 U.S. 478, 508 (1978).
405. 474 U.S. 193 (1985).
406. *Id.* at 207–08.
407. 420 U.S. 308 (1975).
408. *Id.* at 320.

Prosecutorial Functions vs. Investigative Acts

The Supreme Court has similarly accorded prosecutors absolute immunity for acts intertwined with judicial proceedings, and rejected absolute immunity for administrative and investigative acts. In several decisions the Court has defined a protected "prosecutorial" act.

In *Imbler v. Pachtman*,[409] the Court held that absolute immunity applied to a prosecutor's action in "initiating a prosecution and in presenting the State's case."[410] Protected by this immunity was the alleged knowing use of false testimony at trial and the alleged deliberate suppression of exculpatory evidence. The Court granted absolute immunity by considering two issues: (1) the availability of immunity at common law, and (2) whether absolute immunity would undermine the goals of § 1983. At common law, prosecutors had immunity from suits based on malicious prosecution and defamation. In addition, immunity properly shields prosecutors from suits by disgruntled criminal defendants and protects their ability to act decisively, and thus does not undermine the goals of § 1983. The Court also stated that qualified immunity would not adequately protect prosecutors. The remedies of professional self-discipline and the criminal law[411] serve as checks to the broad discretion of prosecutors.

In *Burns v. Reed*,[412] the challenged actions included both investigative and prosecutorial acts: (1) the prosecutor's legal advice to police officers about the use of hypnosis as an investigative tool and the existence of probable cause to arrest the plaintiff; and (2) the prosecutor's misleading presentation of a police officer's testimony at a probable-cause hearing for the issuance of a search warrant.[413] The Supreme Court held that the prosecutor had absolute immunity for his participation at the probable-cause hearing[414] but only qualified immunity for his legal advice to the police.[415]

---

409. 424 U.S. 409 (1976).
410. *Id.* at 431.
411. *Id.* at 430–31.
412. 500 U.S. 478 (1991).
413. *Id.* at 487.
414. *Id.* at 492.
415. *Id.* at 496.

Absolute immunity is necessary only when there is "interference with . . . conduct closely related to the judicial process."[416] Whereas at the hearing the prosecutor acted as an "advocate for the State"[417] and his appearance was "intimately associated with the judicial phase of the criminal process,"[418] "advising the police in the investigative phase" was not sufficiently close to the judicial process.[419] Moreover, it would be "incongruous" to afford prosecutors absolute immunity "from liability for giving advice to the police, but to allow police officers only qualified immunity for following the advice."[420]

The Supreme Court reiterated the need to link the challenged action to the judicial process in *Buckley v. Fitzsimmons*.[421] It held that the prosecutor did not have absolute immunity for two challenged actions: conspiring "to manufacture false evidence that would link [the plaintiff's] boot with the boot print the murderer left on the front door" and conducting a press conference defaming the plaintiff shortly before the defendant's election and the grand jury's indictment of the plaintiff.[422] In neither instance did the prosecutor act as an "advocate" for the state.[423]

The *Buckley* Court attempted to create a bright line for distinguishing prosecutorial acts from investigative acts: "A prosecutor neither is, nor should consider himself to be, an advocate before he has probable cause to have anyone arrested."[424] The Court limited this rule by stating that the presence or absence of probable cause is not dispositive of the issue of absolute immunity; even after a prosecutor has probable cause, he may perform investigative work protected only by qualified immunity.[425] Under the facts of the case, the prosecutor did not have probable cause before he allegedly manufactured false evidence, and thus was not entitled to absolute immunity. With respect to the second claim, a press conference, even if an important part of a prosecutor's job, is not functionally tied to the judicial process.

---

416. *Id.* at 494.
417. *Id.* at 491.
418. *Id.* at 492.
419. *Id.* at 493.
420. *Id.* at 495.
421. 113 S. Ct. 2606, 2614–15 (1993).
422. *Id.* at 2615.
423. *Id.* at 2617–18.
424. *Id.* at 2616.
425. *Id.* at 2616 n.5.

In *Kalina v. Fletcher*,[426] however, the Court did not refer to the presence or absence of probable cause in deciding whether actions performed by a prosecutor were protected by absolute immunity. Instead it focused on whether the prosecutor had filed sworn or unsworn pleadings with the court. The Court held that the prosecutor had absolute immunity for filing two unsworn pleadings—an information and a motion for an arrest warrant—but not for the act of personally vouching for the truthfulness of facts set forth in a document called a "Certification for Determination of Probable Cause." Traditionally, police officers and complaining witnesses perform the latter function when they personally attest to the truthfulness of statements in support of a warrant. The Court refused to extend absolute immunity to this act because it interpreted the common law as not providing this type of broad immunity.

Other Official Acts Protected by Absolute Immunity

In addition to legislative, judicial, and prosecutorial functions, the Supreme Court has recognized that police officers testifying during a trial also merit absolute immunity.[427] Testifying is an act inextricably intertwined with the judicial process.

Although the Court has repeatedly stated that absolute immunity does not apply to an office but rather to the function performed, in *Nixon v. Fitzgerald*[428] the Court held that official acts by a President are protected by absolute immunity.[429] It held that, in this *Bivens* action,[430] President Nixon had absolute immunity for the firing of an employee.[431]

---

426. 118 S. Ct. 502 (1997).

427. Briscoe v. LaHue, 460 U.S. 325, 344–49 (1983).

428. 457 U.S. 731 (1982).

429. The immunity is a "functionally mandated incident of the President's unique office, rooted in the constitutional tradition of the separation of powers and supported by our history." *Id.* at 749.

430. A *Bivens* action is one filed against a federal official for an alleged constitutional violation. *See* Bivens v. Six Unknown Named Agents, 403 U.S. 388 (1971).

431. In contrast, in *Clinton v. Jones*, 117 S. Ct. 1636, 1639 (1997), the Court rejected President Clinton's unique request for a deferral of his trial and discovery, a request that did not assert absolute immunity, but rather used the policy of absolute immunity to argue for postponement. The Court held that it would not defer discovery and a trial for alleged sexual harassment that occurred before Clinton became President.

The Court has rejected applying absolute immunity in other circumstances: a public defender's conspiracy with a state judge[432] and a governor's decision to deploy the National Guard at Kent State University.[433]

In sum, application of the absolute immunity defense depends on the need to safeguard the judicial and legislative processes. When rejecting absolute immunity as a defense for administrative and investigative actions, the Court has often stated that these actions will be adequately protected by the defense of qualified immunity, which is at the heart of most § 1983 litigation.

432. Dennis v. Sparks, 449 U.S. 24 (1980).
433. Scheuer v. Rhodes, 416 U.S. 232 (1974).

Chapter 7

Qualified Immunity from Damages

The affirmative defense of qualified immunity may provide officials[434] with two types of protection. First, it functions as a defense to liability when the actions allegedly taken by officials did not violate "clearly established" law.[435] If the law was not clearly established when officials acted, qualified immunity bars an award of damages, but it does not preclude the granting of injunctive relief.[436] Second, qualified immunity may provide officials with an "immunity from suit"[437] by relieving them from the burdens both of discovery and a trial.

The seminal decision of *Harlow v. Fitzgerald*[438] and its progeny provide guidance in determining the clarity of the law. Procedural motions under the Federal Rules of Civil Procedure protect officials' immunity from suit.

---

434. When plaintiffs sue "private" individuals, qualified immunity may not be a defense: private prison guards, who had limited supervision by the government, did not have qualified immunity for their actions in restraining a prisoner, *Richardson v. McKnight*, 117 S. Ct. 2100, 2109 (1997); a private creditor, who invoked unconstitutional state "replevin, garnishment, and attachment statutes" with the aid of state officials, did not have qualified immunity, *Wyatt v. Cole*, 504 U.S. 158, 159 (1992). In these cases, however, the Court did not decide whether these private defendants acted under color of law, the first element for a prima facie § 1983 lawsuit.

435. Harlow v. Fitzgerald, 457 U.S. 800, 818 (1982).

436. Behrens v. Pelletier, 116 S. Ct. 834, 842 (1996).

437. Mitchell v. Forsyth, 472 U.S. 511, 526 (1985).

438. 457 U.S. 800 (1982).

Defense to Liability

In *Harlow*, the Supreme Court held that "governmental officials performing discretionary function[s] generally are shielded from liability for civil damages insofar as their conduct does not violate clearly established statutory or constitutional rights of which a reasonable person would have known."[439] The purpose of this objective standard was to resolve insubstantial claims prior to discovery. The *Harlow* Court significantly modified the prior standard by holding that subjective bad faith was no longer relevant to the qualified immunity defense. Eliminating the factual issue of subjective good faith would facilitate resolution of this defense prior to discovery.

In establishing the objective standard for qualified immunity, the Court weighed the plaintiffs' interests in having their constitutional rights vindicated against the public's need for governmental officials to perform their duties. Requiring officials to act in subjective good faith had resulted in their incurring the burdens of discovery and litigation for suits that were clearly unmeritorious. An objective standard, the Court declared, is in the public's interest because it appropriately safeguards the officials' decision-making processes and allows officials more time for public service.

When applying the objective qualified immunity standard to § 1983 claims, courts are to resolve two issues: (1) Has the plaintiff stated a violation of a constitutional or federal statutory right?;[440] and (2) If so, was that right clearly established, i.e., were the "contours of the right . . . sufficiently clear that a reasonable official would understand that what [he or she] is doing violates that right"?[441] Resolution of the latter issue depends on the degree of correspondence between the facts of the case under consideration and the facts from prior cases decided at the time the official acted. If there is a close correspondence, then the officials would not receive qualified immunity because the case law would have put the official on notice that his or her conduct was clearly unconstitutional.

---

439. *Id.* at 818. It also created a limited exception for officials who could prove that they neither knew nor should have known of the clearly established right. *Id.* In practice, litigation has focused on the standard; rarely has the exception applied.

440. Siegert v. Gilley, 500 U.S. 226, 232 (1991).

441. Anderson v. Creighton, 483 U.S. 635, 640 (1987).

A decision by the Supreme Court is not necessary to establish this notice.[442] However, conflict among the courts of appeals may indicate that the law was not "clearly established."[443]

"Clearly Established Law" as Applied to Fourth Amendment Claims

In *Malley v. Briggs*[444] and *Anderson v. Creighton*,[445] the Supreme Court addressed Fourth Amendment claims and explained that "clearly established" law does not refer to general principles of law. In these decisions, the Court stated that qualified immunity applies if a reasonable officer under the same circumstances could not have known his or her conduct was illegal. This is a question of law for the courts to decide.[446]

In *Malley*, the Court held that police officers acting pursuant to an invalid arrest warrant may nevertheless assert the defense of qualified immunity.[447] The Court recognized two standards of reasonableness: conduct unreasonable under the Fourth Amendment could still be objectively reasonable for the purpose of qualified immunity.[448] It noted that it had similarly recognized two standards of reasonableness when creating the objective good-faith exception to the exclusionary rule.[449] Under that exception, even if officers got evidence by committing an unreasonable search or seizure, in violation of the Fourth Amendment, the evidence could nevertheless be used in the case-in-chief if they acted in "objective" good faith. This objective good faith standard asks whether a "reasonably well-trained officer" with a "reasonable knowledge of what the law prohibits" would have known that the challenged action violated the Fourth Amendment.[450]

442. United States v. Lanier, 117 S. Ct. 1219, 1226 (1997).

443. *Id.* at 1226–27.

444. 475 U.S. 335 (1986).

445. 483 U.S. 635 (1987).

446. Elder v. Holloway, 510 U.S. 510, 516 (1994) (remanding and holding that the court of appeals must consider (de novo on appeal) relevant case law in resolving question of whether an asserted federal right was "clearly established").

447. Malley v. Briggs, 475 U.S. 335, 343–46 (1986).

448. *Id.* at 344–45.

449. *Id.* at 344 (citing United States v. Leon, 468 U.S. 897 (1984) (objective reasonableness is the standard for a search done pursuant to an invalid warrant)).

450. United States v. Leon, 468 U.S. 897 (1984).

The *Anderson* Court affirmed this dual standard of reasonableness[451] as it addressed whether police officers could assert qualified immunity for a warrantless search of the plaintiff's home. The Court conceded that the general principles of Fourth Amendment law are clear: a warrantless search of an individual's home, absent probable cause and exigent circumstances, is unreasonable. The Court explained, however, that these general principles did not determine whether the officers had immunity. Whether the officers violated "clearly established" law requires consideration of the "contours of a [constitutional] right."[452] The proper inquiry is whether the contours of the right were "sufficiently clear that a reasonable official would understand that what he [did] violate[d] that right."[453]

The *Anderson* Court gave little guidance as to how to assess the "contours" of a right. It stated that a police officer may "reasonably, but mistakenly, conclude that probable cause is present."[454] Similarly, a police officer may reasonably but mistakenly conclude that exigent circumstances exist. If there is a "legitimate question" as to the unlawfulness of the conduct, qualified immunity applies.[455] The decision further states, "[T]he very action in question, however, [need not have] been previously held unlawful," but if "in light of preexisting law the unlawfulness [was] apparent," then qualified immunity does not apply.[456]

Immunity from Discovery and Trial

In addition to being a defense to liability, qualified immunity may also shield officials both from discovery and a trial. Determining when offi-

---

451. Anderson v. Creighton, 483 U.S. 635, 636–41 (1986).

452. *Id.* at 640.

453. *Id.* The Supreme Court adhered to this approach in its later per curiam decision in *Hunter v. Bryant*, 112 S. Ct. 534 (1992). In *Hunter*, the Court explained that the proper inquiry is whether the officials "acted reasonably under settled law in the circumstances, not whether another, or more reasonable interpretation of events can be constructed. . . ." *Id.* at 537. *See generally* McCleary v. Navarro, 504 U.S. 966, 967 (1992) (White, J., dissenting from the denial of certiorari, joined by Chief Justice Rehnquist and Justices O'Connor and Thomas) (stating that the appropriate qualified immunity question is whether "a reasonable officer could have thought that he had acted in accordance with the Constitution, and not whether an officer would have acted otherwise").

454. *Anderson*, 483 U.S. at 641.

455. *Id.*

456. *Id.*

cials may properly invoke this immunity from suit requires courts to interpret the Federal Rules of Civil Procedure in light of the qualified immunity defense. In several decisions, the Supreme Court has offered procedural guidance.

Motion to Dismiss

In the typical motion to dismiss under Fed. R. Civ. P. 12(b)(6), a court assumes that the plaintiff's allegations are true and determines whether these allegations state a violation of a constitutional or federal statutory right. If they do not, then the court dismisses the claim.

Many courts also consider motions to dismiss under Rule 12(b)(6) when officials raise qualified immunity as a defense.[457] The difficulty of considering qualified immunity at this time in the lawsuit is that qualified immunity is an affirmative defense,[458] and Fed. R. Civ. P. 8(c) requires affirmative defenses such as qualified immunity to be raised in an answer. The Court recently stated: "We refused to change the Federal Rules governing pleading by requiring the plaintiff to anticipate the immunity defense."[459]

The Supreme Court implied that some of the Federal Rules of Civil Procedure provide officials with the opportunity to gather information about a plaintiff's case, making a "heightened pleading" standard unnecessary. (Under that standard,[460] plaintiffs had to plead with particularity, even though the Federal Rules of Civil Procedure only require notice

457. *See, e.g.*, Fortner v. Thomas, 983 F.2d 1111, 1114–15 (3d Cir. 1988); *but see* Triad Assocs., Inc. v. Robinson, 10 F.3d 492 (7th Cir. 1993).

458. Gomez v. Toledo, 446 U.S. 635 (1980).

459. Crawford-El v. Britton, 523 U.S. —, 118 S. Ct. 1584, 1595 (1998) (citing with approval Gomez v. Toledo, 446 U.S. 635, 639–40 (1980)). The Court also expressed its reluctance to legislate pleading requirements: "our cases demonstrate that questions regarding pleading, discovery, and summary judgment are most frequently and most effectively resolved either by the rulemaking process or the legislative process"). *Id.*

460. *See, e.g.*, Siegert v. Gilley, 500 U.S. 226, 235 (1991) (Kennedy, J., concurring) (stating that "[t]he heightened pleading standard is a necessary and appropriate accommodation between the state of mind component of malice and the objective test that prevails in qualified immunity analysis as a general matter"); Branch v. Tunnel, 14 F.3d 449, 457 (9th Cir. 1994), *cert. denied*, 114 S. Ct. 2704 (1995) (court is not free to revisit the issue of heightened pleading because the decision in *Leatherman v. Tarrant County Narcotics Intelligence & Coordination Unit*, 113 S. Ct. 1160 (1993), specifically left the issue open); *but see* Triad Assocs., Inc. v. Robinson, 10 F.3d 492 (7th Cir. 1993) (heightened pleading does not apply when there is a motion to dismiss).

pleading.) First, Fed. R. Civ. P. 7(a) gives district courts discretion to order a reply to an official's answer, which properly raises qualified immunity as an affirmative defense.[461] Second, Fed. R. Civ. P. 12(e) allows officials to move for a "more definite statement."[462] Both of these rules accomplish the goal of a heightened pleading standard because the granting of the motions requires plaintiffs to "'put forward specific, nonconclusory factual allegations' . . . to survive a prediscovery motion for dismissal or summary judgment."[463] Thus, even when the underlying constitutional claim requires proof of an official's intent, these rules adequately safeguard an official's immunity from unnecessary discovery.[464]

In motions under Rule 12(b)(6), courts have decided two issues: whether the allegations state a claim and whether the law was "clearly established," an issue arising from the qualified immunity affirmative defense. According to the Supreme Court, when motions properly raise the qualified immunity defense, courts are to first decide whether the plaintiff has stated a claim before addressing the "clearly established" law question.[465] In practice, both the Supreme Court[466] and lower courts[467]

---

461. *Crawford-El*, 118 S. Ct. at 1596. The Fifth Circuit had previously recognized how Fed. R. Civ. P. 7 eliminates the need for a "heightened pleading" standard:

> First, the district court must insist that a plaintiff suing a public official under § 1983 file a short and plain statement of his complaint, a statement that rests on more than conclusions alone. Second, the court may, in its discretion, insist that a plaintiff file a reply tailored to an answer pleading the defense of qualified immunity. Vindicating the immunity doctrine will ordinarily require such a reply, and a district court's discretion not to do so is narrow. . . . The district court may ban discovery at this threshold pleading stage and may limit any necessary discovery to the defense of qualified immunity. The district court need not allow any discovery unless it finds that plaintiff has supported his claim with sufficient precision and factual specificity to raise a genuine issue as to the illegality of defendant's conduct at the time of the alleged acts. Even if such limited discovery is allowed, at its end, the court can again determine whether the case can proceed and consider any motions of summary judgment under Rule 56.

Schultea v. Wood, 47 F.3d 1427, 1433–34 (5th Cir. 1995) (en banc).

462. *Crawford-El*, 118 S. Ct. at 1596.

463. *Id.* at 1596–97 (quoting Siegert v. Gilley, 500 U.S. 226, 236 (1991) (Kennedy, J., concurring in judgment)).

464. *Id.* at 1596.

465. Siegert v. Gilley, 500 U.S. 226, 232 (1991); *accord* County of Sacramento v. Lewis, 523 U.S. —, 118 S. Ct. 1708, 1714 n.5 (1998). In *County of Sacramento*, the Supreme Court stated in a footnote: "the first step is to identify the exact contours of the underlying right said to have been violated." *Id.* It explained that if courts were instead to assume a constitutional violation and address the second step, whether the law was sufficiently clear to put officials on notice that their actions were unconstitutional, "standards of official conduct would tend to remain uncertain, to the detriment both of officials and indi-

have often *not* addressed the first issue. Instead they have simply assumed a violation when deciding the clarity of the law issue.

Motions for Summary Judgment Before and After Discovery

The Supreme Court's purpose in creating an objective standard of reasonableness to evaluate qualified immunity was to resolve insubstantial claims prior to discovery.[468] Officials may raise the qualified immunity defense in summary judgment motions under Federal Rule of Civil Procedure 56(c)[469] both before[470] and after discovery.[471] Under Rule 56(c), summary judgment is permitted if there are no disputed material facts and the person is entitled to judgment as a matter of law.

Summary judgment motions before discovery are possible because the qualified immunity defense is not only a defense to liability but also an "immunity from suit" in some circumstances.[472] Under *Harlow*, discovery is not to occur if the plaintiff has not alleged a violation of clearly established law.[473]

If, however, the plaintiff has alleged a violation of clearly established law, and the defendant alleges actions that a reasonable officer could have thought were lawful, then courts must grant discovery tailored to the immunity question.[474] Even when the underlying constitutional claim sued on requires a plaintiff to prove an official's intent, courts are *not* to

---

viduals." *Id*. The Court twice stated that its two-step process is "the better approach." *Id*.

466. *See, e.g.*, Hunter v. Bryant, 502 U.S. 224 (1991) (per curiam) (granting qualified immunity after assuming officers violated the Constitution).

467. *See, e.g.*, DiMeglio v. Haines, 45 F.3d 790, 795–99 (4th Cir. 1995) (stating that *Siegert* does not compel courts to first decide whether plaintiff has stated a claim); *but see* Manzano v. South Dakota Dep't of Soc. Servs., 60 F.3d 505, 510 n.2 (8th Cir. 1995) (stating that Eighth Circuit has consistently adhered to *Siegert's* requirement to first address whether plaintiff stated a claim).

468. Harlow v. Fitzgerald, 457 U.S. 800, 815–16 (1982).

469. Fed. R. Civ. P. 56(c).

470. Anderson v. Creighton, 483 U.S. 635, 646 n.6 (1987); Harlow v. Fitzgerald, 457 U.S. 800, 818–19 (1982).

471. Behrens v. Pelletier, 116 S. Ct. 834, 842 (1996).

472. Mitchell v. Forsyth, 472 U.S. 511, 526 (1985) (plurality opinion).

473. *Harlow*, 457 U.S. at 818.

474. *Anderson*, 483 U.S. at 646 n.6.

impose a "heightened standard of proof."[475] Instead, they are to tailor discovery by using procedures provided in Fed. R. Civ. P. 26.[476]

Under Rule 26, district courts may limit the number of depositions and interrogatories, the length of depositions, the "time, place, and manner of discovery,"[477] and the sequence of discovery. In addition, district courts may limit discovery to an issue that may resolve the lawsuit before allowing discovery as to an official's intent. For example, an official "may move for partial summary judgment on objective issues that are potentially dispositive and are more amenable to summary disposition than disputes about the official's intent, which frequently turn on credibility assessments."[478] In contrast, Fed. R. Civ. P. 56(f) gives district courts discretion to postpone deciding an official's motion for summary judgment if discovery is necessary to establish "facts essential to justify the [plaintiff's] opposition."[479]

In addition, district courts safeguard officials' right to be free from frivolous lawsuits by imposing sanctions under Fed. R. Civ. P. 11 or granting dismissal under 28 U.S.C. § 1915(e)(2), a statute permitting dismissal of "frivolous or malicious" in forma pauperis suits.[480] In short, district courts have "broad discretion in the management of the factfinding process."[481]

After discovery has occurred, officials may raise a second summary judgment motion. In *Mitchell v. Forsyth*,[482] the Court explained that if the complaint alleged a violation of "clearly established law" and "discovery fail[ed] to uncover evidence that the defendant in fact committed those acts," the defendant is entitled to qualified immunity.[483] In many situations, however, material facts are disputed.

Summary judgment would nevertheless be possible if, interpreting the facts in the light most favorable to the plaintiff, the court determines that the alleged facts do not state a violation of clearly established law.[484] In

---

475. Crawford-El v. Britton, 523 U.S. —, 118 S. Ct. 1584, 1595 (1998).

476. *Id.* at 1597.

477. *Id.*

478. *Id.*

479. *Id.* at n.20.

480. *Id.* at 1598 (quoting 28 U.S.C. § 1915(e)(2) (Supp. 1998)).

481. *Id.*

482. 472 U.S. 511 (1985).

483. *Id.* at 526.

484. *Anderson*, 483 U.S. at 646 n.6.

this situation, the immunity defense relieves officials from the burdens of trial, protecting their "immunity from suit."[485] If, however, the facts as interpreted in the light most favorable to the plaintiff indicate a violation of clearly established law, and the discovery indicates material facts are in dispute, then summary judgment is not possible. At this point, the "immunity from suit" is properly lost and the case must go to trial.

Role of the Judge and Jury

Once courts properly deny summary judgment because material facts are in dispute, it is for the jury to determine the facts and for the court to determine whether the law was "clearly established" when the official acted. In *Hunter v. Bryant*,[486] the Court held that "[i]mmunity *ordinarily should be decided by the court long before trial*."[487] It criticized the lower court for "routinely" placing the issue of immunity "in the hands of the jury."[488]

To resolve the legal question of whether the law was clearly established, some courts[489] have used special verdicts under Rule 49(a) to have a jury resolve the factual dispute.[490] After the jury makes its findings, a court can then determine the clarity of the law at the time the official acted.[491] In addition, courts may consider renewed motions for qualified immunity. These motions may occur after the plaintiff has presented her case, at the close of both sides, after the jury's special verdict, or in a motion for a new trial.[492] Resolution is possible during these trial stages if the defendant is entitled to judgment as a matter of law.

485. *Mitchell*, 472 U.S. at 526.

486. 502 U.S. 224 (1991).

487. *Id.* at 228.

488. *Id.*

489. *See, e.g.*, Mahoney v. Kesery, 976 F.2d 1054, 1058 (7th Cir. 1992); Floyd v. Laws, 929 F.2d 1390 (9th Cir. 1991).

490. Fed. R. Civ. P. 49(a).

491. *See, e.g.*, Warren v. Dwyer, 906 F.2d 1339, 1348 (11th Cir. 1991), *cert. denied*, 111 S. Ct. 431 (1990).

492. *See, e.g.*, Warlick v. Cross, 969 F.2d 303, 308 (7th Cir. 1992).

Interlocutory Appeals

Jurisdiction under 28 U.S.C. § 1291

When a district court denies an official's motion for qualified immunity, the official, in some circumstances, may take an interlocutory appeal.[493] The jurisdictional basis for this appeal is 28 U.S.C. § 1291,[494] a statute that creates a procedural right to an interlocutory appeal from a "final" decision.[495] Whether an appeal is proper depends on whether the district court's order is a "final" decision within the meaning of § 1291.

Generally, an order is a "final" decision if the district court denied qualified immunity by determining that the law was "clearly established" at the time the official acted;[496] it is not final if the district court only determined that the plaintiff had offered sufficient evidence to avoid summary judgment in favor of the official.[497] Because the Supreme Court has stated that appellate courts may not create a rule limiting officials to one interlocutory appeal, appellate courts must decide whether a particular order is a final decision.[498]

Determining finality requires courts to examine the "immunity from suit" aspect of *Harlow* and the collateral order doctrine, a judicially created doctrine interpreting what finality means in § 1291.[499] In *Mitchell*, a plurality of the Court interpreted *Harlow* as establishing an "immunity from suit" because it held that discovery should not proceed until the plaintiff has alleged a violation of clearly established law. In short, not only was qualified immunity a defense to liability, it was an immunity from *unnecessary* discovery and trials.

When a district court denies an official's claim to qualified immunity, it may be erroneously subjecting the official either to the burden of discovery or a trial. *Mitchell* stated that a district court's determination that

---

493. An official may also seek interlocutory review from orders denying absolute immunity. Mitchell v. Forsyth, 472 U.S. 511, 528–30 (1985).

494. 28 U.S.C. § 1291 (1993). Section 1291 provides in part: "The courts of appeal . . . shall have jurisdiction of appeals from all final decisions of the district courts of the United States. . . ."

495. Johnson v. Fankell, 117 S. Ct. 1800, 1804 (1997).

496. Behrens v. Pelletier, 116 S. Ct. 834, 842 (1996); Mitchell v. Forsyth, 472 U.S. 511, 530–35 (1985).

497. Johnson v. Jones, 115 S. Ct. 2151, 2159 (1995).

498. *Behrens*, 116 S. Ct. at 840.

499. Mitchell v. Forsyth, 472 U.S. 511, 530 (1985).

the law was clearly established is a final order because it satisfies all three elements of the collateral order doctrine: (1) the order "conclusively determine[s] the disputed question"; (2) the order "resolve[s] an important issue completely separate from the merits of the action"; and (3) the order would be effectively "unreviewable from a final judgment."[500]

Thus, if an appellate court were to reverse the district court's order that the law was clearly established, the official would have immunity from this claim. (Qualified immunity protects officials as long as they did not violate clearly established law.) The appellate court would have conclusively resolved an important issue that was separate from the merits. Without this appellate review, the official's "immunity from suit" claim would be "unreviewable."

In contrast, the Court in *Johnson v. Jones*[501] held that an appellate court lacks jurisdiction to review the single issue whether the district court erred in determining that there are material facts in dispute. [502] Such an order is not appealable because it is not separate from the merits, the second requirement of the collateral order doctrine. The Supreme Court recognized three policy reasons for not reviewing these orders: [503] (1) district courts have expertise in determining whether there are material disputed facts; (2) appellate courts might revisit the issue in a later appeal; and (3) appeals of this type of order may cause unnecessary delay.

An order, however, that raises both issues—the clarity of the law and whether material facts are disputed—may be appealable. In *Behrens v. Pelletier*,[504] the Supreme Court explained how appellate courts are to review this type of interlocutory order: "*Johnson* permits [an official] to claim on appeal that all of the conduct which the District Court deemed sufficiently supported for purposes of summary judgment met the *Harlow* standard of 'objective legal reasonableness.'"[505] Thus, if the district court determined that material facts were in dispute and decided that the law was clearly established, an appellate court is to examine the clarity of

---

500. *Id.* at 525–27. The collateral order doctrine has its origins in *Cohen v. Beneficial Industrial Loan Corp.*, 337 U.S. 541 (1949).
501. 515 U.S. —, 115 S. Ct. 2151 (1995).
502. *Id.* at 2159.
503. *Id.* at 2158.
504. 116 S. Ct. 834 (1996).
505. *Id.* at 842 (quoting *Johnson*, 115 S. Ct. at 2159).

law issue, an issue for which it has jurisdiction under the collateral order doctrine, by using the district court's assumed facts.

If the district court "did not identify the particular charged conduct that it deemed adequately supported,"[506] then the appellate court "may have to undertake a cumbersome review of the record to determine what facts the district court, in the light most favorable to the nonmoving party, likely assumed."[507] Such a review thus requires the courts to review depositions and other evidence raised in response to a summary judgment motion.

Other jurisdictional questions for interlocutory appeals

When officials seek interlocutory appeals, district courts and appellate courts may encounter important related jurisdictional issues: jurisdiction when appeals are frivolous and jurisdiction under the doctrine of pendent appellate jurisdiction.

Under the traditional divestiture rule, once an official files a timely notice of appeal, a district court loses jurisdiction.[508] However, a district court may retain jurisdiction after denying an official's motions for summary judgment raising qualified immunity if it certifies the appeal as frivolous.[509] After writing an order explaining how the appeal is frivolous,[510] the district court may proceed with the lawsuit. Nevertheless, the appellate court also has jurisdiction to determine whether it has jurisdiction after the district court has declared the appeal to be frivolous.[511] This "dual jurisdiction"—in the district court and the appellate court—is similar to the dual jurisdiction present when criminal defendants seek interlocutory appeals from orders denying their motions raising the Fifth Amendment protection from double jeopardy.[512] In both situations, district courts may proceed.

---

506. *Id.*

507. *Id.* (quoting *Johnson*, 115 S. Ct. at 2159).

508. *See, e.g.*, United States v. LaMere, 951 F.2d 1106, 1107 (9th Cir. 1991).

509. The Supreme Court explicitly approved of this practice in *Behrens*, 116 S. Ct. at 841. Courts of appeals have supervisory powers to "establish summary procedures . . . to weed out frivolous claims." *Id.*

510. *See generally* United States v. Kress, 58 F.3d 370, 372 (8th Cir. 1995) (stating that after a criminal defendant files an interlocutory appeal from an order denying his motion based on the Fifth Amendment double jeopardy clause, district court may retain jurisdiction by writing an order explaining why appeal is frivolous).

511. *See, e.g.*, Dickerson v. McClellan, 37 F.3d 251, 252 (6th Cir. 1994).

512. *Behrens*, 116 S. Ct. at 841.

Another common jurisdictional question arises from officials asking appellate courts to decide whether the district court erred in deciding that material facts were in dispute. Under § 1291, appellate courts do not have jurisdiction after *Johnson v. Jones*.[513] Yet, under the doctrine of pendent appellate jurisdiction, some courts have decided this issue.[514]

Pendent appellate jurisdiction is a discretionary doctrine that permits appellate courts to decide an issue for which they do not have jurisdiction if that issue is inextricably intertwined with an issue for which they have jurisdiction.[515] In the immunity context, an appellate court has jurisdiction under § 1291 to decide whether the district court erred in deciding that the law was clearly established; it has discretionary jurisdiction to append to this issue whether the district court erred in deciding that material facts were in dispute. However, in *Johnson*, the Court suggested that the appellate court would be "unlikely" to use pendent appellate jurisdiction to review the district court's determination as to the facts.[516]

---

513. 515 U.S. —, 115 S. Ct. 2151 (1995).

514. *See, e.g.*, McMillian v. Johnson, 88 F.3d 1554 (11th Cir. 1996), *amended*, 101 F.3d 1363, *cert. denied*, 117 S. Ct. 2514 (1997).

515. *See, e.g.*, Clinton v. Jones, 117 S. Ct. 1636, 1651 n.41 (1997); Johnson v. Jones, 115 S. Ct. 2151, 2159 (1995); Swint v. Chambers County Comm'n, 115 S. Ct. 1203, 1211–12 (1995).

516. *Johnson*, 115 S. Ct. at 2159.

Chapter 8

Procedural Defenses

Accrual, Statutes of Limitations, and Tolling Rules

Although § 1983 provides a cause of action for violations of constitutional and federal statutory rights, it does not describe the applicable statutes of limitations, nor does it detail accrual and tolling rules. When § 1983 does not address important litigation issues, the Supreme Court has often looked to 42 U.S.C. § 1988,[517] which specifies that if the federal law is "deficient," state law will apply as long as it is "not inconsistent with the Constitution and the laws of the United States."[518]

Although application of § 1988 does not result in one applicable federal rule, the Supreme Court has looked to this statute to resolve issues related to statutes of limitations as well as tolling rules. Under § 1988, a state's statute of limitations relating to personal injury is applicable to § 1983 litigation.[519] If a state has multiple statutes relating to personal injury, then the applicable limitation is the one found in the general or residual statute.[520] State tolling provisions similarly apply to § 1983 litigation.

---

517. 42 U.S.C. § 1988 (1993) provides as follows:

> The jurisdiction in civil and criminal matters conferred on the district courts . . . shall be exercised and enforced in conformity with the laws of the United States, so far as such laws are suitable to carry the same into effect; but in all cases where they are not adapted to the object, or are deficient in the provisions necessary to furnish suitable remedies . . . , the common law, as modified and changed by the constitution and statutes of the State wherein the court having jurisdiction . . . , so far as the same is not inconsistent with the Constitution and the laws of the United States, shall be extended . . . .

Id.

518. *Id.*
519. Wilson v. Garcia, 471 U.S. 261 (1985).
520. Owens v. Okure, 488 U.S. 235, 249–50 (1989).

The issue of accrual is more complex. The courts of appeal generally agree that the accrual of a claim is a federal issue. The Supreme Court in *Chardon v. Fernandez*[521] held that courts should assess accrual from the date the employer notifies an employee of an adverse decision, not the date of dismissal.[522] In assessing the applicable date, the Supreme Court "takes a hard line on when civil rights claims for relief accrue. If there is more than one plausible alternative, the Supreme Court appears to be strongly inclined to pick the earlier date."[523]

Claim and Issue Preclusion

When a federal court has to consider the effect of a prior state court judgment in § 1983 litigation, the relevant statute is 28 U.S.C. § 1738. The issue centers on applicable federal common law of preclusion. Both claim preclusion (res judicata) and issue preclusion (collateral estoppel) apply to § 1983 litigation.[524]

Section 1738 provides that the "judicial proceedings of any court of any State shall have the same full faith and credit in every court within the United States . . . as they have by law or usage in the courts of such State."[525] Claim preclusion prevents "parties or their privies from relitigating issues that were or could have been raised"[526] in the action in which a court has rendered a final judgment. Issue preclusion bars relitigation of an issue of fact or law that was necessary to the prior judgment in "a different cause of action involving a party to the first case."[527]

The Supreme Court has limited the application of issue preclusion for state court judgments under certain circumstances: (1) "the party against whom an earlier court decision is asserted did not have a full and fair opportunity to litigate the claim or issue decided by the first court"; (2) "controlling facts or legal principles have changed significantly since the

---

521. 454 U.S. 6 (1981).

522. *Id.* at 8.

523. Martin A. Schwartz & John E. Kirklin, 1C Section 1983 Litigation: Claims & Defenses, § 12.4, at 13 (3d ed. 1997).

524. Migra v. Warren City Sch. Dist. Bd. of Educ., 465 U.S. 75 (1984) (claim preclusion); Haring v. Prosise, 462 U.S. 306 (1983) (issue preclusion).

525. 28 U.S.C. § 1738 (1993).

526. *See, e.g.,* Allen v. McCurry, 449 U.S. 90, 94 (1980).

527. *Id.*

state-court judgment"; and (3) "special circumstances warrant an exception to the normal rules of preclusion."[528]

Because § 1738 applies to "judicial proceedings," it does not apply to arbitration decisions.[529] Preclusion is more complex, however, when the prior decision was rendered by an administrative body. In *University of Tennessee v. Elliott*,[530] the Supreme Court held "that when a state agency acting in a judicial capacity . . . resolves disputed issues of fact properly before it which the parties have had an adequate opportunity to litigate, . . . federal courts must give the agency's fact finding the same preclusive effect to which it would be entitled in the State's courts." [531] This federal common-law rule of preclusion focuses attention on the nature of the proceeding, a state's rule of preclusion, and its fact finding. Although this rule seems contrary to the purposes of § 1983 as articulated in *Monroe v. Pape*,[532] the Court nevertheless concluded that Congress did not intend to broadly limit § 1738.[533]

---

528. *Haring*, 462 U.S. at 313–14 n.7.
529. McDonald v. City of West Branch, 466 U.S. 284 (1984).
530. 478 U.S. 788 (1986).
531. *Id.* at 799.
532. 365 U.S. 167 (1961).
533. *Id.* at 180.

Chapter 9
Abstention Doctrines

The Supreme Court has described a federal court's obligation to adjudicate claims properly within its jurisdiction as "virtually unflagging." [534] Accordingly, "[a]bstention from the exercise of federal jurisdiction is the exception, not the rule,"[535] and the Supreme Court has limited the circumstances appropriate for abstention. Four abstention doctrines apply to § 1983 litigation in federal court: *Pullman*,[536] *Burford*,[537] *Younger*,[538] and *Colorado River*.[539]

Pullman *Abstention*

In *Railroad Commission of Texas v. Pullman Co.*,[540] plaintiffs sought to enjoin the commission from enforcing a duly promulgated order requiring all railroad sleeping cars in the state of Texas to be under the control of a person having the rank of conductor.[541] At the time, porters on Pullmans were African-Americans; conductors were Caucasians. Plaintiffs assailed the order on both state law and federal constitutional grounds.[542]

The Supreme Court held "that when a federal constitutional claim is premised on an unsettled question of state law, the federal court should

---

534. Colorado River Water Conservation Dist. v. United States, 424 U.S. 800, 817–18 (1976).

535. *Id.* at 813.

536. Railroad Comm'n of Texas v. Pullman Co., 312 U.S. 496 (1941).

537. Burford v. Sun Oil Co., 319 U.S. 315 (1943).

538. Younger v. Harris, 401 U.S. 37 (1971).

539. *Colorado River*, 424 U.S. at 800.

540. 312 U.S. 496 (1941).

541. *Id.* at 497–98.

542. *Id.* at 498.

stay its hand in order to provide the state courts an opportunity to settle the underlying state-law question and thus avoid the possibility of unnecessarily deciding a constitutional question."[543] Thus, the district court should have deferred its decision until the Texas court decided whether the commission had authority under state law to issue the order. If the commission had no such authority, there would be no need to address the federal constitutional issue.[544]

Pullman abstention is applicable only when the issue of state law is unsettled and when the state statute is "fairly subject to an interpretation which will render unnecessary or substantially modify the federal constitutional question."[545] Under *Pullman* abstention, a district court generally retains jurisdiction over the case, but stays its proceedings while the state court adjudicates the issue of state law. Thus, *Pullman* abstention does not "involve the abdication of jurisdiction, but only the postponement of its exercise."[546]

In *England v. Louisiana State Board of Medical Examiners*,[547] the Court set out the procedures to be followed when *Pullman* abstention is invoked.[548] A party has the right to return to the district court for a final determination of the party's claim once the party has obtained the authoritative state-court construction of the state law in question.[549] A party can, but need not, expressly reserve this right, and in no event will the right be denied "unless it clearly appears that he voluntarily . . . fully litigated his federal claim in the state courts."[550] A party may elect to forego the right to return to federal court by choosing to litigate the federal constitutional claim in state court.[551]

543. Harris County Comm'rs Court v. Moore, 420 U.S. 77, 83 (1975) (interpreting *Pullman*).

544. *Pullman*, 312 U.S. at 501.

545. Harman v. Forssenius, 380 U.S. 528, 534–35 (1965).

546. Harrison v. N.A.A.C.P., 360 U.S. 167, 177 (1959).

547. 375 U.S. 411 (1964).

548. An alternative to the procedures outlined in *England* exists in those states that have "certification" statutes allowing a federal appeals court or district court to "certify" a question of unsettled state law to the highest court of the state for a decision. The availability of certification has a great impact on the time and cost involved in *Pullman* abstention. *See generally* Erwin Chemerinsky, Federal Jurisdiction § 12.3 (1994).

549. *England*, 375 U.S. at 417.

550. *Id.* at 421–22.

551. *Id.* at 419. If a party so elects, the Supreme Court has held that, even in § 1983 cases, the sole fact that the state court's decision may have been erroneous will not be

In *Arizonans for Official English v. Arizona*,[552] the Supreme Court suggested that, where available, state certification procedures be used instead of *Pullman* abstention. State certification procedures allow federal courts to directly certify unsettled, dispositive questions of state law to the highest court of the state for authoritative construction. The Court explained:

> Certification today covers territory once dominated by a deferral device called "Pullman abstention" . . . . Designed to avoid federal-court error in deciding state-law questions antecedent to federal constitutional issues, the *Pullman* mechanism remitted parties to the state courts for adjudication of the unsettled state-law issues. If settlement of the state-law question did not prove dispositive of the case, the parties could return to the federal court for decision of the federal issues. Attractive in theory because it placed state-law questions in courts equipped to rule authoritatively on them, *Pullman* abstention proved protracted and expensive in practice, for it entailed a full round of litigation in the state-court system before any resumption of proceedings in federal court. . . . Certification procedure, in contrast, allows a federal court faced with a novel state-law question to put the question directly to the State's highest court, reducing the delay, cutting the cost, and increasing the assurance of gaining an authoritative response.[553]

Burford *Abstention*

In *Burford v. Sun Oil Co.*,[554] the plaintiff sought to enjoin the enforcement of an order of the Texas Railroad Commission permitting the drilling of some wells on a particular Texas oil field. The order was challenged as a violation of both state law and federal constitutional law.[555] The Texas legislature had established a complex, thorough system of administrative and judicial review of the commission's orders, concentrating all direct review of such orders in the state court of one county.[556] The state scheme evidenced an effort to establish a uniform policy with respect to the regulation of a matter of substantial local concern. The Court found that "[t]hese questions of regulation of the industry by the

---

sufficient to lift the bar to relitigation of federal issues decided after a full and fair hearing in state court. Allen v. McCurry, 449 U.S. 90, 101 (1980).

552. 117 S. Ct. 1055 (1997).
553. *Id.* at 1073.
554. 319 U.S. 315 (1943).
555. *Id.* at 317.
556. *Id.* at 324, 326.

state administrative agency . . . so clearly involve basic problems of Texas policy that equitable discretion should be exercised to give the Texas courts the first opportunity to consider them."[557]

Thus, where complex administrative procedures have been developed in an effort to formulate uniform policy in an area of local law, "a sound respect for the independence of state action requires the federal equity court to stay its hand."[558] Unlike *Pullman* abstention, *Burford* abstention does not anticipate a return to the federal district court. The federal court dismisses the action in favor of state administrative and judicial review of the issues, with "ultimate review of the federal questions . . . fully preserved" in the Supreme Court.[559]

In *New Orleans Public Service, Inc. v. Council of City of New Orleans (NOPSI)*,[560] the Court clarified that "[w]hile *Burford* is concerned with protecting complex state administrative processes from undue federal interference, it does not require abstention whenever there exists such a process, or even in all cases where there is a 'potential for conflict' with state regulatory law or policy."[561] In *NOPSI* the Court emphasized that the primary concern underlying *Burford* abstention is the avoidance of federal disruption of "the State's attempt to insure uniformity in the treatment of an essentially local problem."[562]

The Court has held that the power to dismiss or remand a case based on *Burford* abstention principles exists only where the relief sought is equitable or otherwise discretionary in nature.[563] Where damages were being sought, the Court found the district court's remand order to be "an unwarranted application of the *Burford* doctrine."[564]

---

557. *Id.* at 332.

558. *Id.* at 341.

559. *Id.* at 333–34.

560. 491 U.S. 350 (1989). *NOPSI* involved a refusal by the New Orleans City Council to allow NOPSI to get a rate increase to cover additional costs that had been allocated to it, along with other utility companies, by the Federal Energy Regulatory Commission for the Grand Gulf Reactor.

561. *Id.* at 362.

562. *Id.* at 364.

563. Quackenbush v. Allstate Ins. Co., 117 S. Ct. 1712, 1728 (1996).

564. *Id.* Given the facts of the case before it, the Court found it unnecessary to decide whether a more limited "abstention-based stay order" would have been appropriate. *Id.*

Younger *Abstention*

In *Younger v. Harris*,[565] the Supreme Court held that a federal district court could not enjoin state criminal proceedings pending in state court when the federal suit was commenced.[566] The Court made clear that its decision was not based on an application of the Anti-Injunction Act.[567] Rather, a basic doctrine of equity dictated that no injunction should be granted "when the moving party has an adequate remedy at law and will not suffer irreparable injury if denied equitable relief."[568] Because the federal plaintiff could raise and vindicate his federal constitutional rights in the course of the state criminal proceeding, an adequate remedy was available in the pending state prosecution. More importantly, the Court emphasized the notion of "comity," or "Our Federalism," a system that guards against undue interference by the national government with "the legitimate activities of the states."[569]

The *Younger* doctrine has been extended substantially beyond the context of prohibiting injunctions against pending state criminal pro-

---

565. 401 U.S. 37 (1971).

566. *Id.* at 41. The Court noted three "extraordinary circumstances" in which a federal court need not defer to pending state court proceedings: first, where the state is engaged in a "bad faith" prosecution in order to harass the federal plaintiff, with no purpose or expectation of obtaining a conviction (*id.* at 49); second, where a state statute is "flagrantly and patently violative of express constitutional prohibitions in every clause, sentence and paragraph, and in whatever manner and against whomever an effort may be to apply" (*id.* at 53–54) (internal quotation marks and citations omitted); finally, where the pending state proceedings will not afford an adequate opportunity to vindicate the federal plaintiff's constitutional rights (*id.* at 48–49). *See, e.g.,* Gibson v. Berryhill, 411 U.S. 564 (1973) (*Younger* held inapplicable because state board of optometry was incompetent, by reason of bias, to adjudicate the issues pending before it). While these three "extraordinary circumstances" were identified as exceptions to the application of *Younger* abstention, as one commentator has noted, "each of them is very limited. *Younger* is not an absolute ban on federal court injunctions, but it is quite close." Erwin Chemerinsky, Federal Jurisdiction § 13.4 (1994).

567. 28 U.S.C. § 2283 (1994) provides:

> A court of the United States may not grant an injunction to stay proceedings in a State court except as expressly authorized by Act of Congress, or when necessary in aid of its jurisdiction, or to protect or effectuate its judgments.

In *Mitchum v. Foster*, 407 U.S. 225 (1972), the Court held that § 1983 is an expressly authorized exception to the Anti-Injunction Act. Thus, *Younger* abstention operates as an independent bar to the enjoining of state court proceedings.

568. *Younger*, 401 U.S. at 43–44.

569. *Id.* at 44.

ceedings. In *Samuels v. Mackell*,[570] the Supreme Court held that in federal cases where a state criminal prosecution had begun prior to the federal suit, "where an injunction would be impermissible under [*Younger*] principles, declaratory relief should ordinarily be denied as well."[571] While the Supreme Court has not directly addressed the question of whether *Younger* applies when a federal plaintiff is seeking only monetary relief with respect to matters that are the subject of a state criminal proceeding,[572] it has implied that *Colorado River* abstention might be appropriate in such situations.[573]

In a number of decisions, beginning with *Huffman v. Pursue, Ltd.*,[574] the Court has extended the application of *Younger* to bar federal interference with state civil proceedings. In *Huffman*, the Court noted that the civil nuisance proceeding at issue in the case was in important respects "more akin to a criminal prosecution than are most civil cases," because

570. 401 U.S. 66 (1971).

571. *Id.* at 73. In *Steffel v. Thompson*, 415 U.S. 452 (1974), the Court addressed the issue of the availability of declaratory relief when no state criminal prosecution is pending. Noting that the relevant principles of equity, comity, and federalism carry little force in the absence of a pending state proceeding, the Court unanimously held that "federal declaratory relief is not precluded when no state prosecution is pending and a federal plaintiff demonstrates a genuine threat of enforcement of a disputed state criminal statute . . . ."*Id.* at 475. The Court's decision in *Steffel*, however, must be read in conjunction with its subsequent decision in *Hicks v. Miranda*, 422 U.S. 332 (1975), holding that where state criminal proceedings are commenced against a federal plaintiff after the federal complaint has been filed but "before any proceedings of substance on the merits have taken place in the federal court," the *Younger* doctrine applies "in full force." *Id.* at 349.

The Court has likewise held that the granting of preliminary injunctive relief (*see* Doran v. Salem Inn, Inc., 422 U.S. 922 (1975)) or permanent injunctive relief (*see* Wooley v. Maynard, 430 U.S. 705 (1977)) is not barred by *Younger* principles when no criminal proceeding is pending.

572. In *Deakins v. Monaghan*, 484 U.S. 193 (1988), the Court held that a district court "has no discretion to dismiss rather than to stay claims for monetary relief that cannot be redressed in the state proceeding." *Id.* at 202.

573. *See* Heck v. Humphrey, 114 S. Ct. 2364, 2373 n.8 (1994) ("[I]f a state criminal defendant brings a federal civil-rights lawsuit during the pendency of his criminal trial, appeal, or state habeas action, abstention may be an appropriate response to the parallel state-court proceedings." (citing *Colorado River*)). The Court held in *Heck* that when a state prisoner seeks damages in a § 1983 suit, the district court must consider whether a judgment in favor of the plaintiff would necessarily imply the invalidity of his conviction or sentence; if it would, the complaint must be dismissed unless the plaintiff can demonstrate that the conviction or sentence has already been invalidated. *Id.* at 2373.

574. 420 U.S. 592 (1975).

the state was a party to the proceeding, and the proceeding itself was in aid of and closely related to criminal statutes.[575] Thus, while refusing to make any general pronouncements as to *Younger's* applicability to all civil litigation, the Court held that the district court "should have applied the tests laid down in *Younger*" in deciding whether to enjoin the state civil nuisance proceeding.[576]

Younger has been applied to prohibit federal court interference with pending state administrative proceedings. In *Middlesex County Ethics Commission v. Garden State Bar Ass'n*,[577] the Court was faced with the question of whether pending state bar disciplinary hearings were subject to the principles of *Younger*. In holding *Younger* applicable, the Court underscored the judicial nature of the proceedings, the "extremely important" state interest involved, and the availability of an adequate opportunity for the representation of constitutional claims in the process.[578]

---

575. *Id.* at 604. In *Moore v. Sims*, 442 U.S. 415 (1979), the Court treated the case as governed by *Huffman* because the state was a party to the state proceedings in question, and the temporary removal of a child in a child abuse context was in aid of and closely related to enforcement of criminal statutes.

576. *Huffman*, 420 U.S. at 607. In *Trainor v. Hernandez*, 431 U.S. 434 (1977), the Court held that the principles of *Younger* and *Huffman* were broad enough to apply to interference by a federal court with ongoing attachment proceedings "brought by the State in its sovereign capacity" to vindicate important state policies. *Id.* at 444. *See also* Juidice v. Vail, 430 U.S. 327, 335 (1977) (holding that principles of "comity" and "federalism" applied to a case where the state was not a party, but where the state's judicial contempt process was involved and the state's interest in the contempt process is of "sufficiently great import to require application of the principles of *Younger*"); Pennzoil Co. v. Texaco Inc., 481 U.S. 1, 13–14 & n.12 (1987) (reversing lower court's granting of federal court injunction against a state court requirement that Texaco post bond in excess of $13 billion in order to prevent the execution of a judgment against it while an appeal was pursued; holding that the rationale of *Younger* applied to this civil proceeding, observing the state's interest in protecting "the authority of the judicial system, so that its orders and judgments are not rendered nugatory"). *But see NOPSI*, 491 U.S. 350, 368 (1989) (holding that *Younger* does not apply to state judicial proceedings "reviewing legislative or executive action").

577. 457 U.S. 423 (1982).

578. In *Ohio Civil Rights Commission v. Dayton Christian Schools, Inc.*, 477 U.S. 619 (1986), the Court emphasized that the application of *Younger* to pending administrative proceedings is fully consistent with the rule that litigants need not exhaust administrative remedies before they can bring a § 1983 suit in federal court (*see* Patsy v. Board of Regents of Fla., 457 U.S. 496 (1982)), because "the administrative proceedings here are coercive rather than remedial[;] began before any substantial advancement in the federal action took place[;] and involve an important state interest." *Ohio Civil Rights Comm'n*, 477 U.S.

Colorado River *Abstention*

In *Colorado River Water Conservation District v. United States*,[579] the Supreme Court confronted the question of what a federal court should do when there are duplicative proceedings occurring in state court. The government had brought suit seeking a declaration of water rights on its own behalf and on behalf of certain Indian tribes.[580] Soon thereafter, a defendant in the federal suit moved to join the United States in a state court proceeding adjudicating the same water rights. The federal district court subsequently dismissed the suit, abstaining in deference to the state court proceedings.[581] Although the Supreme Court found that none of the so-called "abstention doctrines" applied to the facts of this case,[582] it held that dismissal was proper "on another ground—one resting not on considerations of state–federal comity or on avoidance of constitutional decisions, as does abstention, but on considerations of wise judicial administration, giving regard to conservation of judicial resources and comprehensive disposition of litigation."[583]

The Court noted the general rule that "the pendency of an action in the state court is no bar to proceedings concerning the same matter in the Federal court having jurisdiction."[584] There are, however, exceptional circumstances that might permit dismissal of a federal suit in the face of concurrent state court proceedings.[585] The Court identified four factors to be considered in determining whether such exceptional circumstances exist: (1) problems created by two courts exercising concurrent jurisdiction over a res; (2) the issue of the relative inconvenience of the federal forum; (3) the goal of avoiding piecemeal litigation; and (4) the order in which the state and federal forums obtained jurisdiction.[586]

---

at 627–28 n.2.

579. 424 U.S. 800 (1976).

580. *Id.* at 805.

581. *Id.* at 806.

582. *Id.* at 813–17.

583. *Id.* at 817 (citing Kerotest Mfg. Co. v. C-O-Two Fire Equip. Co., 342 U.S. 180, 183 (1952)).

584. *Colorado River*, 424 U.S. at 817 (citing McClellan v. Carland, 217 U.S. 268, 282 (1910)).

585. *Id.* at 818.

586. *Id.*

In *Moses H. Cone Memorial Hospital v. Mercury Construction Co.*,[587] the Court underscored the need for exceptional circumstances before a federal court surrenders its jurisdiction over a case on the ground that there is a duplicative proceeding occurring in state court.[588] In addition, the Court announced that another factor to be given great weight in the balancing of considerations is the presence of a question of federal law. [589]

While the Court left open the question of whether the proper course to take when employing *Colorado River* abstention is a stay or a dismissal without prejudice, it is clear that "resort to the federal forum should remain available if warranted by significant change of circumstances."[590] A dismissal or stay of a federal action is improper unless the concurrent state action has jurisdiction to adjudicate the claims at issue in the federal suit.[591]

In *Wilton v. Seven Falls Co.*,[592] the Supreme Court resolved a conflict among the circuits regarding the standard to be applied by a district court in deciding whether to stay a declaratory judgment action in deference to parallel state proceedings. The Court held that "[d]istinct features of the Declaratory Judgment Act . . . justify a standard vesting district courts with greater discretion in declaratory judgment actions than that permitted under the 'exceptional circumstances' test of *Colorado River* and *Moses H. Cone* . . . . In the declaratory judgment context, the normal principle that federal courts should adjudicate claims within their jurisdiction yields to considerations of practicality and wise judicial administration."[593]

---

587. 460 U.S. 1 (1983). The case involved parallel state and federal proceedings addressing the issue of whether a contract between the parties was subject to arbitration.

588. *Id.* at 25, 26.

589. *Id.* at 23.

590. Arizona v. San Carlos Apache Tribe, 463 U.S. 545, 570 n.21 (1983). To safeguard against the running of the statute of limitations should the state litigation leave some issues unresolved, the preferable course would be to stay, rather than dismiss the federal action. *See* Wilton v. Seven Falls Co., 115 S. Ct. 2137, 2143 n.2 (U.S. 1995) (noting that "where the basis for declining to proceed is the pendency of a state proceeding, a stay will often be the preferable course, insofar as it assures that the federal action can proceed without risk of a time bar if the state case, for any reason, fails to resolve the matter in controversy").

591. *San Carlos Apache Tribe*, 463 U.S. at 560.

592. 115 S. Ct. 2137 (1995).

593. *Id.* at 2138–43. The Court found that the discretionary standard announced in *Brillhart v. Excess Insurance Co. of America*, 316 U.S. 491 (1942), had not been supplanted

A stay order granted under *Colorado River* is final and immediately appealable.[594] However, an order refusing abstention under *Colorado River* is "inherently tentative" and is not immediately appealable under the collateral order doctrine.[595]

by the "exceptional circumstances" test of *Colorado River* and *Moses H. Cone*. *Brillhart*, like *Wilton*, involved an insurer seeking a federal declaratory judgment of nonliability in the face of a state court coercive suit seeking coverage under the policy. *See also* NYLife Distributors, Inc. v. Adherence Group, Inc., 72 F.3d 371, 382 (3d Cir. 1995) (holding that "the discretionary standard enunciated in *Brillhart* governs a district court's decision to dismiss an action commenced under the interpleader statute during the pendency of parallel state court proceedings").

594. Moses H. Cone Mem'l Hosp. v. Mercury Constr. Co., 460 U.S. 1, 10 (1983).

595. Gulfstream Aerospace Corp. v. Mayacamas Corp., 485 U.S. 271, 278 (1988).

Chapter 10
Remedies

Compensatory Damages

The full range of common-law remedies is available to a plaintiff asserting a claim under § 1983. Legal relief may take the form of nominal, compensatory, as well as punitive damages. "When § 1983 plaintiffs seek damages for violations of constitutional rights, the level of damages is ordinarily determined according to principles derived from the common law of torts."[596] The Supreme Court has stressed, however, that "[t]he rule of damages . . . is a federal rule responsive to the need whenever a federal right is impaired."[597]

Compensatory damages generally fall into one of three categories: special, general, or nominal damages. Special damages relate to specific pecuniary losses, such as lost earnings, medical expenses, and loss of earning capacity. General damages include compensation for physical pain and suffering, as well as emotional distress. Nominal damages reflect the violation of a right with no proven actual injury.

In *Carey v. Piphus*,[598] the Supreme Court held that "although mental and emotional distress caused by the denial of procedural due process itself is compensable under § 1983, neither the likelihood of such injury nor the difficulty of proving it is so great as to justify awarding compensatory damages without proof that such injury actually was caused."[599] Thus, actual damages will not be presumed in a procedural due process case and, without proof of damages, the plaintiff will be entitled only to

---

596. Memphis Community Sch. Dist. v. Stachura, 477 U.S. 299, 306 (1986).
597. Sullivan v. Little Hunting Park, Inc., 396 U.S. 229, 240 (1969).
598. 435 U.S. 247 (1978).
599. *Id.* at 264.

"nominal damages not to exceed one dollar."[600] The Court noted in *Carey* that the primary purpose of the damages remedy in § 1983 litigation is "to compensate persons for injuries caused by the deprivation of constitutional rights."[601]

The Court relied on *Carey* and extended its holding to a case involving the violation of a plaintiff's First Amendment rights in *Memphis Community School District v. Stachura.*[602] In *Stachura*, the Supreme Court held that "damages based on the abstract 'value' or 'importance' of constitutional rights are not a permissible element of compensatory damages" in § 1983 cases.[603] The problem identified in *Stachura* was that the district court's jury instructions allowed for an award of damages that was neither compensatory nor punitive, but was based solely on the perceived "value" or "importance" of the particular constitutional right violated.[604] The Court distinguished the line of common-law voting rights cases in which presumed damages have been awarded "for a nonmonetary harm that cannot easily be quantified."[605] Thus, while presumed damages ordinarily will not be available in § 1983 actions, presumed damages may be appropriate "[w]hen a plaintiff seeks compensation for an injury that is likely to have occurred but difficult to establish."[606]

Punitive Damages

A plaintiff may be awarded punitive damages against an individual defendant "when the defendant's conduct is shown to be motivated by evil motive or intent, or when it involves reckless or callous indifference to the federally protected rights of others."[607] As is the case with compensatory damages, federal law governs the availability of punitive damages in a federal civil rights action under § 1983.[608] A local government unit is immune from punitive damages under § 1983.[609]

---

600. *Id.* at 267.
601. *Id.* at 254.
602. 477 U.S. 299 (1986).
603. *Id.* at 310.
604. *Id.* at 310 n.13.
605. *Id.* at 311 & n.14.
606. *Id.* at 310–11.
607. Smith v. Wade, 461 U.S. 30, 56 (1983).
608. *See, e.g.,* Wulf v. City of Wichita, 883 F.2d 842, 867 (10th Cir. 1989).
609. City of Newport v. Fact Concerts, Inc., 453 U.S. 247, 271 (1981).

In *Pacific Mutual Life Insurance Co. v. Haslip*,[610] the Supreme Court established guidelines for determining whether punitive damages awarded under *state* law violated substantive due process. The Court focused on the jury instructions as to the purpose of punitive damages, the adequacy of procedures for the trial court's review of the award, and the adequacy of state appellate court review.[611] The jury instructions approved by the court in *Haslip* informed the jury that the purpose of punitive damages was deterrence and retribution. Furthermore, the jury was advised that it must consider the character and degree of the wrong as shown by the evidence and the necessity of preventing similar wrong. Finally, the jury was informed that the imposition of punitive damages was not compulsory.[612]

The Court found the procedures that had been established by the Supreme Court of Alabama for post-trial scrutiny of punitive awards ensured meaningful and adequate review of punitive damages by the trial court. The factors to be considered by the trial court included the culpability of the defendant's conduct, as well as the desirability of discouraging others from similar conduct.[613] The final safeguard against irrational punitive awards was in the criteria applied by the state appellate court. In assessing the reasonableness of an award of punitive damages, the following criteria were used by the state appellate court and approved by the Supreme Court:

> (a) whether there is a reasonable relationship between the punitive damages award and the harm likely to result from the defendant's conduct as well as the harm that actually has occurred; (b) the degree of reprehensibility of the defendant's conduct, the duration of that conduct, the defendant's awareness, any concealment, and the existence

---

610. 499 U.S. 1 (1991).

611. *Id.* at 16–18. *See also* BMW of North Am., Inc. v. Gore, 116 S. Ct. 1589, 1604 (1996) ("As in *Haslip*, we are not prepared to draw a bright line marking the limits of a constitutionally acceptable punitive damages award. Unlike that case, however, we are fully convinced that the grossly excessive award imposed in this case transcends the constitutional limit."); TXO Prod. Corp. v. Alliance Resources Corp., 509 U.S. 443, 453–54, 462 (1993) (agreeing that several of the Court's opinions have recognized that the Fourteenth Amendment places substantive limits on punitive damages awards, but rejecting the argument that the $10 million punitive damages award in this case was so "grossly excessive" that it violated substantive due process).

612. *Haslip*, 499 U.S. at 19.

613. *Id.*

and frequency of similar past conduct; (c) the profitability to the defendant of the wrongful conduct and the desirability of removing that profit and of having the defendant also sustain a loss; (d) the "financial position" of the defendant; (e) all the costs of litigation; (f) the imposition of criminal sanctions on the defendant for its conduct, these to be taken in mitigation; and (g) the existence of other civil awards against the defendant for the same conduct, these also to be taken in mitigation.[614]

The majority of courts of appeals agree that punitive damages may be appropriate even where only nominal damages are awarded.[615] While *Haslip* reinforces the principle that juries must take the financial condition of the defendant into account when assessing the punitive damages award, there remains disagreement as to whether the plaintiff or the defendant has the burden of producing evidence as to the financial position of the defendant.[616]

Survival and Wrongful Death Actions Under § 1983

As noted in Chapter 8 (Procedural Defenses), where § 1983 does not provide suitable remedies for constitutional violations, the federal courts are instructed to turn to state law "so far as the same is not inconsistent with the Constitution and laws of the United States."[617] In *Robertson v. Wegmann*,[618] the Supreme Court held that state law on survivorship of

---

614. *Id.* at 21–22. While the Supreme Court has not reviewed a case raising a claim of excessiveness in a punitive damages award where the award was made in a federal court on a federal cause of action, at least one court of appeals has applied the analysis set out in *Haslip* to assess the constitutionality of punitive damages awards made pursuant to federal law in federal courts. *See* Morgan v. Woessner, 997 F.2d 1244, 1255 (9th Cir. 1993) ("The principles of *Haslip* are applicable . . . to punitive damages imposed by federal courts for violations of federal law.").

615. *See, e.g.,* King v. Macri, 993 F.2d 294, 297, 298 (2d Cir. 1993) (citing cases).

616. *Compare* King v. Macri, 993 F.2d 294, 298 (2d Cir. 1993) (burden on defendant to present evidence of financial circumstances at trial) *and* Zarcone v. Perry, 572 F.2d 52, 56 (2d Cir. 1978) (burden on defendant), *with* Morgan v. Woessner, 997 F.2d 1244, 1259 (9th Cir. 1993) (burden on plaintiff with respect to state law claims) *and* Keenan v. City of Philadelphia, 983 F.2d 459, 483, 484 (3d Cir. 1992) (Higginbotham, J., dissenting) (plaintiff should have burden of producing evidence of defendant's financial condition).

617. *See* 42 U.S.C. § 1988(a) (1994).

618. 436 U.S. 584 (1978).

claims should control so long as that state law is not generally "inhospitable to survival of § 1983 actions . . . [and] has no adverse effect on the policies underlying § 1983."[619] Although the Court held applicable a state law that caused the § 1983 action to abate in that case, it indicated that the situation might be different where the "deprivation of federal rights caused death."[620]

The Supreme Court has not resolved the issue of whether wrongful death claims may be pursued under § 1983. As one court has noted, this question "has 'generated considerable confusion and disagreement,' over which the circuits have divided."[621] In a leading circuit case, *Brazier v. Cherry*,[622] the Court of Appeals for the Fifth Circuit made no distinction between the state's survival statutes and its wrongful death statutes for purposes of the § 1983 action, concluding that "utilization of local death and survival statutes" served the goal of making federal civil rights legislation "fully effectual."[623]

In *Jefferson v. City of Tarrant*,[624] the Supreme Court had granted certiorari to decide whether the Alabama Wrongful Death Act "governs recovery when a decedent's estate claims, under . . . Section 1983 that the death in question resulted from a deprivation of federal rights,"[625] but dismissed the appeal for lack of jurisdiction.

Injunctive Relief

To obtain injunctive relief in federal court, a plaintiff must demonstrate "the likelihood of substantial and immediate irreparable injury, and the inadequacy of remedies at law."[626] In *City of Los Angeles v. Lyons*,[627] the plaintiff sought to enjoin the future use of a chokehold to which he had been subjected when stopped by the police. The Court held that Lyons

---

619. *Id.* at 594.

620. *Id.*

621. Rhyne v. Henderson County, 973 F.2d 386, 390 (5th Cir. 1992) (quoting Crumpton v. Gates, 947 F.2d 1418, 1420 (9th Cir. 1991)). *See generally* Stephen L. Steinglass, *Wrongful Death Actions and Section 1983*, 60 Ind. L.J. 559 (1985). *Compare* Shaw v. Stroud, 13 F.3d 791 (4th Cir. 1994), *with* Bell v. City of Milwaukee, 746 F.2d 1205 (1984).

622. 293 F.2d 401 (5th Cir.), *cert. denied*, 368 U.S. 921 (1961).

623. *Id.* at 409.

624. 118 S. Ct. 481 (1997).

625. *Id.* at 484.

626. O'Shea v. Littleton, 414 U.S. 488, 502 (1974).

627. 461 U.S. 95 (1983).

did not satisfy the prerequisites for seeking equitable relief. Speculation or conjecture that he might be subjected to the chokehold at some time in the future was not sufficient to demonstrate "any real or immediate threat that the plaintiff [would] be wronged again."[628] Furthermore, the legality of the challenged conduct could be litigated in the plaintiff's claim for damages. Thus, there existed an adequate remedy at law.

The Court in *Lyons* suggested that the plaintiff would have had standing to seek injunctive relief if he had alleged either that "*all* police officers in Los Angeles *always* choke any citizen with whom they happen to have an encounter," or that "the City ordered or authorized police officers to act in such manner."[629] Following *Lyons*, courts of appeals have found standing to seek injunctive relief where the conduct to be enjoined has been authorized by policy or practice.[630] In determining what constitutes sufficient "official authorization" to satisfy the *Lyons* requirement for seeking injunctive relief, courts should look to cases interpreting the scope of "official policy or custom" in the context of asserting claims for damages against a governmental unit.[631]

Declaratory Relief

Under the Declaratory Judgment Act,[632] given the existence of "a case of actual controversy within its jurisdiction," a federal court "may declare the rights and other legal relations of any interested party seeking such declaration."[633] Declaratory relief is available even when an adequate remedy at law exists.

A declaratory judgment rules on the lawfulness of the policy or conduct challenged by the plaintiff, but, unlike injunctive relief, does not require that the court become engaged in intrusive oversight of governmental activity. A plaintiff need not make a showing of irreparable injury

---

628. *Id.* at 111. The Court relied on its prior decisions in O'Shea v. Littleton, 414 U.S. 488 (1974) and Rizzo v. Goode, 423 U.S. 362 (1976).

629. *Lyons*, 461 U.S. at 106 (emphasis in original).

630. *See, e.g.,* Church v. City of Huntsville, 30 F.3d 1332 (11th Cir. 1994); International Molders & Allied Workers v. Nelson, 799 F.2d 547 (9th Cir. 1986).

631. Monell v. Department of Soc. Servs., 436 U.S. 658 (1978). *See generally* "Chapter 5: Governmental and Supervisory Liability," *supra.*

632. 28 U.S.C. § 2201 (1994).

633. *Id.*

to get declaratory relief.[634] A declaratory judgment, like any other final judgment, has full res judicata effect.[635]

Abstention Doctrines and Statutory Bars to Relief Under § 1983

As explained in Chapter 9 (Abstention Doctrines), there are certain circumstances under which a federal court will abstain from exercising its jurisdiction in a § 1983 action. In such cases, plaintiffs may be forced to pursue their remedies under state law. In addition, the Tax Injunction Act[636] prohibits federal courts from enjoining "the assessment, levy or collection of any tax under State law where a plain, speedy and efficient remedy may be had in the courts of such state." In *California v. Grace Brethren Church*,[637] the Court held that the Tax Injunction Act applied to federal declaratory judgment suits challenging the constitutionality of state tax laws.[638] In *Fair Assessment in Real Estate Ass'n v. McNary*,[639] the Court found that the principle of comity operated to preclude a damages action under § 1983 contesting the validity of a state tax system.[640] Finally, in *National Private Truck Council, Inc. v. Oklahoma Tax Commission*,[641] the Court resolved a conflict among the state courts "as to whether, in tax cases, state courts must provide relief under § 1983 when adequate remedies exist under state law."[642] The Court held that "[w]hen a litigant seeks declaratory or injunctive relief against a state tax pursuant to § 1983 . . . state courts, like their federal counterparts, must refrain from granting federal relief under § 1983 when there is an adequate legal remedy."[643]

---

634. Steffel v. Thompson, 415 U.S. 452, 466–67 (1974).
635. *See, e.g.,* Green v. Mansour, 474 U.S. 64 (1986).
636. 28 U.S.C. § 1341 (1988).
637. 457 U.S. 393 (1982).
638. *Id.* at 407–11.
639. 454 U.S. 100 (1981).
640. *Id.* at 116.
641. 515 U.S. 582 (1995).
642. *Id.* at 585–86.
643. *Id.* at 592.

Attorney's Fees

The Civil Rights Attorney's Fees Awards Act of 1976[644] provides that a prevailing party in actions brought under specified civil rights statutes, including § 1983, may be entitled to an award of attorney's fees as part of the costs of litigation. The Act has generated a tremendous volume of litigation and is treated as the subject of a separate monograph on attorney's fees.[645]

Prison Litigation Reform Act (PLRA)[646]

In any action involving prisoners' rights, there are likely to be substantial limitations placed on the availability and scope of the remedies sought. While a discussion of the various provisions of the PLRA is beyond the scope of this monograph, the importance of consulting the Act in appropriate cases cannot be overemphasized. For example, the PLRA precludes the bringing of a civil action by a prisoner "for mental or emotional injury suffered while in custody without a prior showing of physical injury."[647] Exhaustion of administrative remedies is required in actions relating to prison conditions.[648] The availability of attorney's fees is significantly restricted.[649] Injunctive relief in prison reform litigation must be

---

644. 42 U.S.C. § 1988(b), *amended by* Pub. L. No. 104-317, Title III, § 309(b), 110 Stat. 3853 (119), provides:

> (b) Attorney's fees
>
> In any action or proceeding to enforce a provision of sections 1981, 1981a, 1982, 1983, 1985, and 1986 of this title, title IX of Public Law 92-318 [20 U.S.C.A. § 1681 et seq.], the Religious Freedom Restoration Act of 1993 [42 U.S.C.A. § 2000bb et seq.], title VI of the Civil Rights Act of 1964 [42 U.S.C.A. § 2000d et seq.], or section 13981 of this title [Violence Against Women Act], the court, in its discretion, may allow the prevailing party, other than the United States, a reasonable attorney's fee as part of the costs, except that in any action brought against a judicial officer for an act or omission taken in such officer's judicial capacity such officer shall not be held liable for any costs, including attorney's fees, unless such action was clearly in excess of such officer's jurisdiction.

645. *See generally* Alan Hirsch & Diane Sheehey, Awarding Attorneys' Fees & Managing Fee Litigation (Federal Judicial Center 1994).

646. On April 26, 1996, Congress enacted the Prison Litigation Reform Act as Title VIII of the Omnibus Consolidated Rescissions and Appropriations Act of 1996, Pub. L. No. 104-134, 110 Stat. 1321 (1996).

647. 42 U.S.C. § 1997e(e) (Supp. 1997). *See, e.g.,* Zehner v. Trigg, 133 F.3d 459, 464 (7th Cir. 1997) (upholding constitutionality of provision).

648. 42 U.S.C. § 1997e(a) (Supp. 1997).

649. 42 U.S.C. §§ 1997e(d)(1)–(4) (Supp. 1997).

narrowly drawn to remedy violations of federal rights.[650] Government officials may seek the immediate termination of all prospective relief that was awarded or approved before the enactment of the PLRA without a finding by the court that "the relief is narrowly drawn, extends no further than necessary to correct the violation of the federal right, and is the least intrusive means necessary to correct the violation of the federal right."[651]

---

650. 18 U.S.C. § 1362(a) (Supp. 1997).

651. 18 U.S.C. § 3626(b)(2). This provision has been the subject of much recent litigation. The courts of appeals that have addressed the constitutionality of the provision have uniformly upheld the section, but the rationales have varied and the issue will no doubt wind its way to the Supreme Court. *See, e.g.,* Inmates of the Suffolk County Jail v. Rouse, 129 F.3d 649 (1st Cir. 1997); Benjamin v. Jacobson, 122 F.3d 1055 (2d Cir. 1997); Gavin v. Branstad, 122 F.3d 1081 (8th Cir. 1997); Plyler v. Moore, 100 F.3d 365 (4th Cir. 1996), *cert. denied*, 117 S. Ct. 2460 (1997). *See also* James v. Lash, 965 F. Supp. 1190 (N.D. Ind. 1997); Jensen v. County of Lake, 958 F. Supp. 397 (N.D. Ind. 1997). One court has struck down the termination provision as violating separation of powers principles. Hadix v. Johnson, 947 F. Supp. 1100 (E.D. Mich. 1996).

Table of Cases

About the Federal Judicial Center

The Federal Judicial Center is the research and education agency of the federal judicial system. It was established by Congress in 1967 (28 U.S.C. §§ 620–629), on the recommendation of the Judicial Conference of the United States.

By statute, the Chief Justice of the United States chairs the Center's Board, which also includes the director of the Administrative Office of the U.S. Courts and seven judges elected by the Judicial Conference.

The Director's Office is responsible for the Center's overall management and its relations with other organizations, including state and foreign courts, through the Interjudicial Affairs Office. Its Systems Innovation & Development Office provides technical support for Center education and research. Commun ications Policy & Design edits, produces, and distributes all Center print and electronic publications, operates the Federal Judicial Television Network, and through the Information Services Office maintains a specialized library collection of materials on judicial administration.

The Court Education Division develops and administers education and training programs and services for nonjudicial court personnel, such as those in clerks' offices and probation and pretrial services offices, and management training programs for court teams of judges and managers.

The Judicial Education Division develops and administers education programs and services for judges, career court attorneys, and federal defender office personnel. These include orientation seminars, continuing education programs, and special-focus workshops.

The Research Division undertakes empirical and exploratory research on federal judicial processes, court management, and sentencing and its consequences, often at the request of the Judicial Conference and its committees, the courts themselves, or other groups in the federal system. Its Federal Judicial History Office develops programs relating to the history of the judicial branch and assists courts with their own judicial history programs.